Credit Risk Management for Derivatives

Ivan Zelenko

Credit Risk Management for Derivatives

Post-Crisis Metrics for End-Users

palgrave
macmillan

Ivan Zelenko
Director, Market and Counterparty Risk
The World Bank
Washington, DC
USA

ISBN 978-3-319-57974-0 ISBN 978-3-319-57975-7 (eBook)
DOI 10.1007/978-3-319-57975-7

Library of Congress Control Number: 2017940380

Printed on acid-free paper

This Palgrave Macmillan imprint is published by Springer Nature
The registered company is Springer International Publishing AG
The registered company address is: Gewerbestrasse 11, 6330 Cham, Switzerland

To Brigitte, to Alexandrine and Maxime, knowing nothing is worth but days spent among us

Foreword

While derivatives have probably been in use long before the term itself was coined, OTC instruments really came into wider knowledge and usage during the 1980s. Since then, they have seen quite explosive growth and have been employed for a variety of purposes. At various times, they have also been viewed as useful instruments, sophisticated means of risk management, and, occasionally, as weapons of mass destruction especially in the aftermath of financial market crises. Partly, this may be that although they are widely used, they are not always fully understood.

In this remarkably lucid and timely book, Ivan brings his deep and long expertise in the area to improve our understanding of these instruments. He describes their use, provides an objective assessment of their role during the financial crisis in 2008, and, most importantly, provides a comprehensive exposition of the developments since that time covering the vast regulatory, market, institutional, and methodological dimensions, including their relationships in a rigorous yet succinct manner.

Ivan shows that while derivatives did not cause the 2008 crisis, their use and the institutional arrangements around their use may have amplified some aspects of the crisis both at the entity and systemic levels. He skillfully draws on this insight to trace the origins of regulatory and institutional changes and the impact these have had on derivatives markets. And even more interestingly, he shows how these changes themselves may have unintended consequences and introduce new sources of risk.

With his strong technical background, Ivan walks the reader through key methodological concepts and approaches to measuring the risks associated with the use of derivatives, including measures of exposure as well as the impact of netting, collateral, credit and debt value adjustments, and the more recent measures for funding valuation adjustments and capital value adjustments. Here, he not only provides the mathematical formulas and their derivation but also describes in a clear manner the purpose of the various measures and an intuitive interpretation of the formulas. And in doing so, he does not shy away from describing the limitations of some these new measures as well as the debates around their meaning and usefulness. This will make the book appealing both to the technically minded and to the participant who may want a more practical understanding.

Ivan complements this technical discussion by weaving in the regulatory and institutional features of derivatives and the extraordinary market developments since the 2008 financial crisis. For example, he addresses the issues associated with market liquidity and borrowing costs, the developments in the benchmark risk-free rates such as LIBOR and their replacements, the development of CCPs and the impacts of initial margin and variation margin.

This book will be useful to variety of audiences. Technical experts will find a comprehensive review and summary, and for them the book will serve as a useful reference. For those who feel they need a better understanding of the measures and uses of derivatives, this book will provide an efficient way to become proficient in both the risk metrics and market practices in the use of derivatives. Even for those not too familiar with the markets and instruments, this could form a useful learning tool as it is so lucidly written; the non-technical reader can even skip some of the mathematical derivations and still absorb the key points and measures. Finally for those who have reached senior executive levels or for board members responsible for risk, this book will bring them up to date on developments in the derivatives market and enable them to ask the right questions in the performance of their functions. This is in short a valuable and highly readable contribution to the body of knowledge on derivatives.

Lakshmi Shyam-Sunder
Vice President and World Bank Group Chief Risk Officer,
The World Bank, 1818 H Street, NW, Washington DC

Acknowledgements

I feel deeply honored to serve at the Word Bank under Lakshmi Shyam-Sunder, Vice President and World Bank Group Chief Risk Officer, and Joaquim Levy, Managing Director and World Bank Group Chief Financial Officer. I am deeply indebted to the Treasury, presently under the leadership of Arunma Oteh, Vice President and World Bank Treasurer, and to the Legal Finance team of the World Bank, for giving me, over a 12-year course, unmatched access to derivatives markets, great collegiality and unforgettable conversations. I also thank all my colleagues in the CRO Vice Presidency of the Bank for their relentless drive to keep market and counterparty risks in check. I would like to extend my warmest thanks to Bertrand Badré, Chief Executive Officer of BlueOrange Capital and formerly World Bank Group Managing Director and Chief Financial Officer. I would like to thank Afsaneh Mashayekhi Beschloss, Graeme Wheeler, Madelyn Antoncic, and Kenneth Lay, who have held the position of World Bank Treasurer over 2000–2015.

Contents

List of Figures

Expanding Valuation Metrics: FVA and KV

List of Tables

Reshaping Derivatives Markets: The Post-2008 Ambition

Abstract This Chapter looks back at the 2008 crisis, and at the destructive forces which, combined together, drastically amplified a dynamic of excess lending and excess leverage to bring down the global financial system and cause the worst economic crisis since 1929. Among them were the opacity and complexity of OTC derivatives. At the G20, or through major reforms like those in the US and in the EU, world leaders posed the foundation of a new market framework with the ambition to de-risk, stabilize and make derivatives markets transparent. Seven years through, with much of this agenda implemented, the chapter reviews the unfinished part, the unintended consequences and the new systemic threats.

Keywords Basel III · Credit risk · Crisis · Derivative markets
Dodd-Frank Act · EMIR · Financial stability · Leverage · Liquidity
OTC over-the-counter · Regulation · Securitization · Shadow banking
Swaps · Systemic risk

1 Derivatives as Mass Destruction Power

1.1 *The Most Severe Crisis Since 1929*

The 2007–2008 crisis only compares to 1929 in terms of severity, depth, and long-lasting impact (Figs. 1 and 2). In 2016, 9 years after its start, the legacy of the crisis still weighs on the world economy. The global

I. Zelenko, *Credit Risk Management for Derivatives*,
DOI 10.1007/978-3-319-57975-7_1

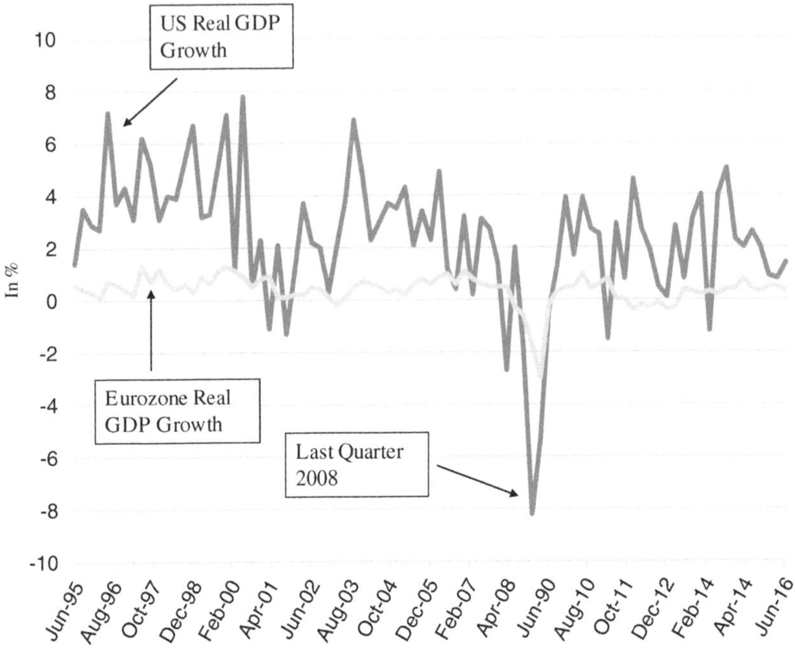

Fig. 1 US and Euro area Real Growth Quarterly Data June 1995–June 2016. *Source* Bloomberg

financial system may have been stabilized for the most part, but the US Fed is only gradually and cautiously moving away from its highly accommodating monetary stance, while the ECB and the Bank of Japan remain committed to negative rates and quantitative easing. In most Western countries, the fall in tax revenues in the aftermath of the 2009 recession, and the emergency spending by governments to rescue and stabilize their banking sector, has brought public debt to historically high levels. The return to "normal" in terms of growth and inflation remains an ongoing concern.

Due to exceptional measures taken—low rates, quantitative easing, and powerful regulatory tightening—and their subsequent very gradual removal, there are still several "pockets" of global and derivative markets that are not back to their "natural" equilibrium.

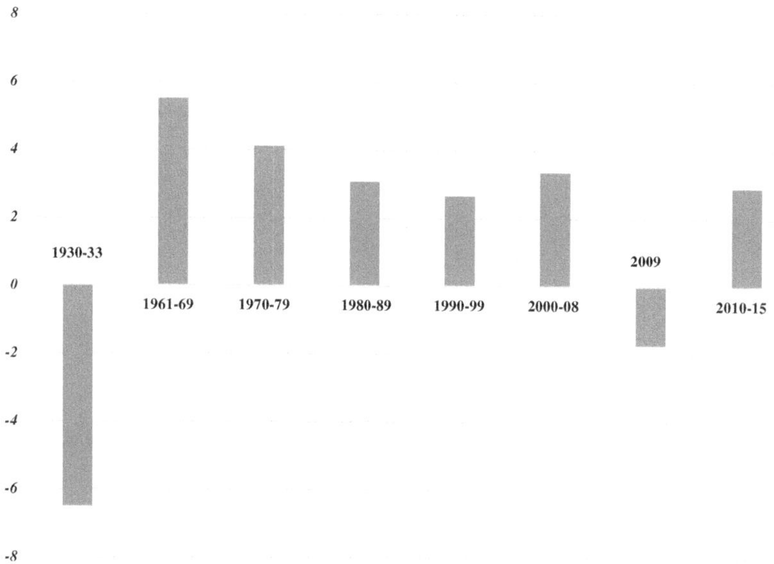

Fig. 2 World GDP Growth (Annual %). *Source* World Bank Annual Data from 1961; JP Morgan

For instance, currency basis swap spreads, which should normally be close to zero but had widened to abnormal levels in 2007 when non-US banks were in urgent need of US dollar liquidity, have not yet reverted back to their equilibrium level (see for instance the 1-year USD Libor–Euribor basis spread in Fig. 3). As of November 2016, the dollar–yen Libor basis spread is in the 60 basis points area and the US dollar Libor–Euribor basis is around 40 basis points.

A major reason for the severity and length of the 2008 crisis lies in the sharp, wide-scale, and damaging banks' losses. Should the banking sector be seriously hurt, a financial crisis would have a long-lasting impact, because the financing of the economy is impaired: *financial stress that is rooted in the banking sector typically has more adverse economic effects than stress in stock markets or exchange rates.*[1] In spite of the prominent role it gives to capital markets, the global financial system still heavily relies on banks, either as lenders or as broker dealers. At the same time, the growing concentration in the banking sector over the past 30 years has

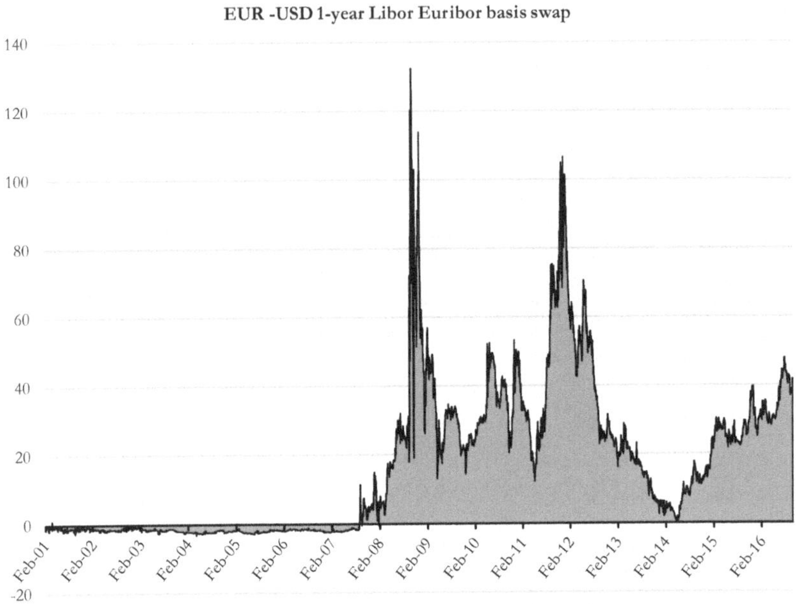

Fig. 3 USD Libor–Euribor 1-year basis swap spread. *Source* Bloomberg, daily data, in basis points

seemingly constituted an irreversible structural evolution. Yet, the emergence of a small set of large universal banks, operating on a global scale, and, in view of their role, having become "systemic" or "too-big-to-fail" has become a key vulnerability of the system. These banks, grouped with the "Systematically Important Financial Institutions" (SIFIs) have become a going concern for economic authorities and regulators.

2007–2008 also compares to 1929 in terms of the magnitude and scope of the governmental response: the re-regulation undertaken since 2009, initiated by the G20 2009 Meeting in Pittsburgh (see Sect. 1.3).

1.2 *The Cause: New Destructive Forces Add to Excess Leverage*

Financial crises tend to follow a generic path, first outlined by the economist Hyman Minsky in 1975. At the onset, an innovation or a new business model appears and gives birth to an active and buoyant market; this new market then attracts many investors and enjoys a strong growth; at a second stage though, there is excess, caused by the attractiveness of this market: excess risk taking, excess search for return; at a further stage, new investments are no longer viable: it is not known immediately to market participants, and investment continues unabated; but this non-viability is eventually revealed: A panic sell-off occurs with all investors attempting to exit at the same time while suffering heavy losses.

The business model, created around 2000, sometimes referred to as: *originate and securitize*, consisted in granting loans to many different borrowers, pooling a large enough number of these loans to benefit from diversification, then making the pool the assets of a new financial entity, a *Special Purpose Vehicle* (SPV), which would issue notes of various ratings and credit risk profiles (*structured notes*) based on the pool. Lightly regulated, these SPVs were performing the traditional functions of a bank, but outside of the balance sheet and of the regulatory framework of a bank; they were a key actor of *shadow banking*. As described by Minsky, *shadow banking* followed the fatal path to excess; loan securitization, implemented in vast amounts, more and more rapidly, and with less and less care, went far beyond the viability line. A name was coined with the riskiest product: *subprime* or structured note backed by suprime loans.

The non-viability was eventually revealed in August 2007, when a fund declared itself unable to honor a redemption because of an "evaporation of liquidity". Rather than with a massive sell-off and price fall, investors were this time confronted with the total disappearance of liquidity, a total paralysis of the loan securitization market: There was no longer any counterparty willing to buy securitized loans. Paralysis was coming not only from fear, but also from the complexity and opacity of the products.

With the securitized loan sector paralyzed, investors turned to the banks that had sold them the products. Strongly committed to their client relationship, and thereby forced to repurchase, banks started re-intermediating securitized loans, and, more worryingly, their risk. Soon enough, the fear, the opacity, and complexity of the securitized products caused liquidity to dry out in the interbank borrowing market: Each bank's creditworthiness was being reassessed. Even as central banks were providing emergency liquidity, a number of several large dealer banks were being suspected of being insolvent.

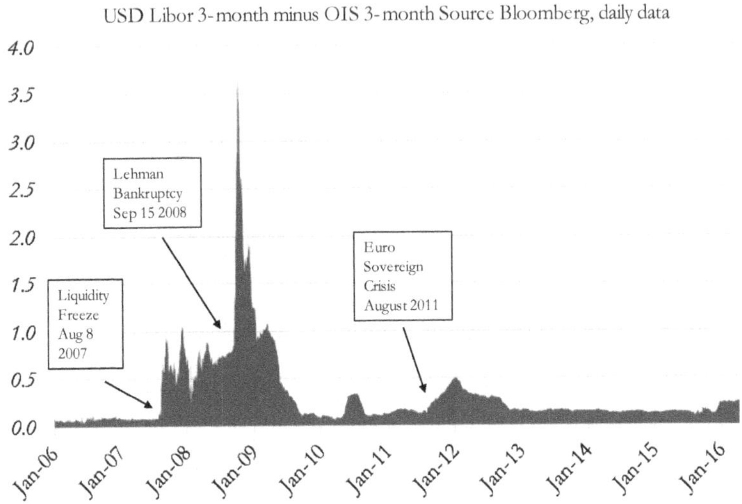

Fig. 4 Breaking Points during the 2007–2008 Crisis and Impact on Libor-OIS 3-month Spread. *Source* Bloomberg, daily data

At the very moment banks were becoming concerned with their ability to fund themselves, another major vulnerability surfaced, the consequence of years of large-scale excess leverage by banks. Looking to maximize profit, banks were funding the assets with short-term wholesale funding, from other banks or fund managers, using secured (repos) or unsecured borrowing (commercial paper or Libor unsecured interbank borrowing). The classic *run on deposits* following the loss of trust in a bank took a new form: Banks were seeing investors running away from all their funding instruments, be they repos or interbank loans. Several banks experiencing severe runs had to be taken over by other banks or by the government.

One among them, Lehman Brothers, for lack of rescue, filed for bankruptcy on September 15, 2008. Because of Lehman's systemic role in the financial market architecture, this precipitated the crisis to a deeper level. In particular, Lehman was a major dealer in the over-the-counter (OTC) derivative market. By their very definition, OTC derivatives are bilateral, idiosyncratic, and often innovative contracts. The unwinding of all Lehman positions and of all the collateral posted or received, and most often re-pledged by Lehman, created unprecedented disorder and turmoil in global financial markets (see Fig. 4).

1.3 The Culprits: Opacity, Complexity, and Derivatives

In 2007, OTC derivatives represented the overwhelming majority of derivatives. The latest big innovation, credit derivatives, was at the very heart of the crisis. Credit derivatives were comprised, for the most part, of credit default swaps (CDS) and of collateralized loan/debt obligations (CLOs/CDOs), the structured securitization products that had generated and facilitated the excess search for yield.

Saying they were at the heart of the crisis does not mean, however, that they were, by themselves, the cause of the crisis. In 2008, testifying before a US Senate Committee, the economist Darrell Duffie was declaring: "it is natural to think of credit derivatives as devices that enabled investors to transfer to each other the losses as they occur, rather than the cause of the losses in the first instance."[2]

There is still a specific danger created by OTC derivatives, which may fundamentally reside in their *over-the-counter*, bilateral, private, and therefore opaque nature. This opacity has two harmful consequences:

- It is impossible for market participants, let alone market supervision authorities, to have an accurate measure of the exposure of market participants—in particular of large SIFIs—and of the overall market, to a particular class of products or risks: The main risk building up in the period prior to 2007 was clearly the US real estate risk but since most of the exposure was through OTC derivatives, and in the shadow banking domain, it was impossible to measure;
- In a situation of bankruptcy, and most especially when the failing entity is a large bank, a SIFI, it is extremely difficult to plan for an orderly unwinding of all bilateral positions—together with the associated collateral—contracted in the form of OTC derivatives. This is due as much to the idiosyncrasy of each position, as to their bilateral nature: No central counterparty can be used to centralize the unwinding process.

Accordingly, the statement of the G20 Meeting in Pittsburgh in September 2009, *Strengthening the International Financial Regulatory System*, was making *improving of OTC derivatives markets* one of its four priorities for a major reform of the system, with a program centered on central clearing[3]:

Box 1: Final Statement of the G20 24–25 September 2009 Meeting: Improving OTC Derivatives Markets

All standardized OTC derivative contracts should be traded on exchanges or electronic trading platforms, where appropriate, and cleared through central counterparties by end-2012 at the latest. OTC derivative contracts should be reported to trade repositories. Non-centrally cleared contracts should be subject to higher capital requirements. We ask the FSB and its relevant members to assess regularly implementation and whether it is sufficient to improve transparency in the derivatives markets, mitigate systemic risk, and protect against market abuse.

In what follows we first take stock of the effort to regain control over the global financial system and of what has been implemented so far, seven years after Pittsburg; we will then turn to the analysis of the effects, to the extent they can be perceived and analyzed over a short period of time.

2 Regaining Control

2.1 The Post-2008 Regulatory Agenda

Soon after the G20 Pittsburgh, the highest rule-making instances in finance worldwide proceeded with turning the G20 list of recommendations into concrete and executable rules.

In July 2010, the US Dodd-Frank Act or *Wall Street reform and Consumer Act* was signed into law. In December 2010, the Basel Committee for Banking and Supervision (BCBS) published the new Basel III framework. Meanwhile, having adopted, as early as September 2009 proposals to strengthen financial regulation, the European Commission (EC) formally launched, in April 2010, the consultation process for revising its core document, the 2004 *Markets in Financial Instruments Directive (MiFID)*. In July 2012, the EC adopted the *European Market Infrastructure Regulation* (EMIR), dealing mostly with OTC derivatives and the requirement to use central clearing counterparties (CCPs). The MiFID II entered into force in July 2014.

The *Dodd-Frank Act* contained an extensive section dealing with OTC derivatives: mandatory clearing of all standardized swaps on

CCPs and mandatory reporting to trade repositories (TRs)—an agenda also conveyed by the European EMIR; mandatory margining rules for uncleared swaps (i.e. swaps not cleared on CCPs) together with a significant tightening of existing collateral practice (see chapter Restating the Role of Collateral on collateral): Rules, in their final form, have been published in the USA in September 2016; similar rules are being finalized, as of November 2016, by EU regulatory agencies; Dodd-Frank also requested the mandatory trading of swaps on exchanges or Swap Execution Facilities (SEFs) when available;

The Dodd-Frank Act was also addressing several key aspects of the crisis: the so-called Volcker Rule was attempting to reestablish a strict separation between: (i) activities banks were pursuing for their clients, as pure brokers, pure market intermediaries; and (ii) trading activities for their own account (proprietary trading), which was proscribed or had to be run in a separate entity. Capital and liquidity requirements were tightened by Dodd-Frank, as were, leverage and short-term borrowing limits. SIFIs were asked to adopt resolution plans or living wills. The surveillance of hedge funds and of securitization vehicles (shadow banking) was strengthened. A framework regulating the compensation of bank executives was established.

Basel III strengthened the Regulatory Capital Requirements of Basel II and introduced three new ratios, added to the capital adequacy ratio as new cornerstones of bank stability destined to reinforce the liquidity of banks and preempt excess leverage.[4] Basel III introduced new tools meant to "reduce procyclicality": forward looking provisioning (based on future expected loss), capital buffers, and a capital surcharge left to the discretion of supervisors as macroprudential tool, so as to prevent credit from growing to excessive levels. Moreover, in dealing with systemic risk, Basel III imposed additional capital charges to SIFIs. Basel III also introduced new capital requirements for derivatives: for uncleared OTC derivatives (an incentive to use CCPs), for wrong-way risk, and for the impact on income of CVA volatility.

The overall spirit of the Pittsburgh agenda was to significantly strengthen the global financial system, increase its resilience and its transparency, and enhance the power of supervision while, at the same time, keeping the effectiveness brought by well-functioning, open, and integrated markets. We may be about to enter into a new phase of amendments to the post-crisis regulation. The US Treasury Secretary, Steve Mnuchin, wants to act on the Executive Order signed by President

Trump on February 3, 2017 and remove parts of Dodd-Frank which inhibit banks from lending. But, while it is too early to analyze the ful scopes of these potential reforms, it seems that the essential features of the reframing of derivatives markets should remain unchanged.

2.2 *The Implementation: Seven Years After Pittsburgh*

Let us now look at the implementation of the post-2008 regulatory agenda. In its first *Report to the G20 on the implementation and effects of the G20 financial regulatory reforms*, published in November 2015, the Financial Stability Board (FSB) gathers the reform agenda around four main themes (see Table 1):

- Strengthening of Financial Institutions (FIs) via new Basel III rules: reinforced capital requirements, new liquidity, and leverage ratios;
- Ending too-big-to-fail: applying stronger requirements to SIFIs, establishing orderly resolution regimes to avoid both the temptation to bail-in or the systemic disruption a la Lehman;
- Making derivatives markets safer, enhancing the structure (CCPs, margining rules) and the transparency (TRs);
- Building a regulatory framework for the shadow banking sector.

The FSB report also identifies areas that merit ongoing attention at the senior level:

- **The implementation in Emerging Markets** (EMs) as well as the impact of the deployment of the post-2008 regulation for EMs, and notably through the spillovers from the implementation in their home jurisdiction of the new framework by global FIs;
- **The limited pool of official sector resources** for carrying out the reform agenda;
- **The need to maintain an open and integrated global financial system**: the FSB, the International Financial Institutions (IFIs), and regulatory bodies monitor the risk of retrenchment in international financial activities and work to maintain an open system;
- **The concern with market liquidity**, which has been raised by market banks: The FSB sees mixed evidence at these points and continues to analyze *"the causes and financial stability consequences of any shifts in market liquidity."*

Table 1 Main Themes of Post-2008 Regulation—High-Level FSB Reporting on Implementation

THEMES	*KEY TOPICS*	*FSB 2015 IMPLEMENTATION REPORT*
Strengthening Financial Institutions (FIs)	Basel III agenda Stronger Capital Requirements New Liquidity and Leverage Ratios Regulatory Framework for Compensation	*Implementation of Basel III capital and liquidity standards has generally been timely and consistent with the Basel framework in most jurisdictions. Banks remain on track to meet these standards. Regulatory frameworks for compensation have been adopted in almost all countries*
Ending "too-big-to-fail" Framework for Systematically Important Financial Institutions (SIFIs)	Stronger Capital & Liquidity Requirements More intensive supervision Effective Resolution Regimes	*Implementation of the policy framework—which consists of higher loss absorbency, more intensive supervision and key attributes of effective resolution—has advanced the most for global systematically important banks. However, substantial work remains in implementing effective resolution regimes*
Making Derivatives Markets more transparent and safer	OTC Derivatives Markets Reforms Central Clearing (CCPs) Margining Rules Trade Repositories	*Implementation of over-the-counter (OTC) derivatives reforms is well underway, although it continues to be uneven and behind schedule. Progress is most advanced in the largest derivatives markets. Trade Repositories (TRs) and central counter-parties are increasingly used*
Transforming Shadow Banking into resilient market-based finance	Framework for lightly regulated entities Hedge Funds, Money Market Funds Securitization markets	*A number of policies were recently finalised in this area (e.g. money market funds, risk alignment of securitization) so implementation is generally at an early stage*

Moreover, the FSB asks for support from G20 Leaders to overcome the following implementation challenges:

- Removing legal barriers to the reporting of OTC derivatives to TRs and to the opening of such reporting to supervisors;
- Promoting cooperation to address duplication of requirements to cross-border derivatives transactions;
- Putting in place legal powers to make foreign resolution actions effective;
- Ensuring that supervisory authorities are adequately resourced.

In sum, the implementation of the Basel III agenda for stronger capital requirements, and for the new liquidity, funding and leverage ratios, has been steadily progressing; the case for managing the systemic risk of SIFIs has advanced, even if resolution regimes are still being implemented within local jurisdictions; on the other hand, the definition of a regulatory framework for the shadow banking sector remains at an early stage.

When it comes to OTC derivatives, the picture is contrasted. CCPs have been implemented for essential segments of OTC derivative trading. Margining regulations are being put into place, with the September 2016 start date in the USA, and implementation in the EU reaching its final stage. But there seems to be challenges in the extension of the area covered by CCPs, and in the transparency agenda pursued via TRs. Meanwhile, swap exchanges or Swap Execution Facilities still constitute a remote objective.

2.3 *The Impact: Curbing Derivatives Credit Risk*

Designing and implementing a new and effective regulation for OTC derivative markets, while preserving their flexibility and their innovative power, may have seemed, at first, an insurmountable task for policy makers. Today, as of June 2017, looking at what has already been accomplished, and at the already tangible benefits, one can reasonably speak of a great achievement, a major step taken in stabilizing derivative markets and the global financial system altogether.

The majority of OTC trading in interest rate swaps (IRSs) and in forward rate agreements, the most standard but also the most widely used products in OTC derivatives markets, has moved to CCPs. As of June 2016, 80% of OTC IRSs and 92% of OTC FRAs were cleared with CCPs. These two categories of OTC derivatives represented 74% of all

OTC derivatives at end-June 2016 (see Table 2). As a result, 62% of all OTC derivatives (i.e., of the total notional amount outstanding) is cleared in CCPs.

The benefit of having such a large proportion in CCPs is straightforward. When they face the CCP, swap users are protected against the risk

Table 2 OTC Derivatives. Evolution of Notional Amount Outstanding and Gross Market Value. *Source* BIS OTC Derivatives Statistics at end-June 2016

In trillions of US dollars	*Global OTC Derivatives Markets*				*Cleared*
Source: BIS end-June 2016	*Notional Amounts Outstanding*		*Gross Market Value*		*with CCPs*
	end-June 2010	end-June 2016	end-June 2010	end-June 2016	end-June 2016
Grand Total	**582.7**	**544.1**	**24.7**	**20.7**	**62%**
Interest Rate Contrats	**478.1**	**437.8**	**18.5**	**16.0**	**75%**
Forward Rate Agreements (FRAs)	60.0	74.7	0.2	0.4	91%
Interest Rate Swaps (IRSs)	367.5	327.4	16.7	14.2	80%
Options	50.5	35.4	1.6	1.4	0%
Foreign Exchange Contracts	**63.0**	**85.7**	**3.2**	**3.6**	**<2%**
Forwards and Swaps	31.9	46.9	1.3	1.7	
Currency Swaps	18.9	25.9	1.4	1.6	
Options	12.1	12.9	0.5	0.3	
Credit Derivatives	**31.4**	**12.0**	**1.7**	**0.4**	**37%**
Credit Default Swaps (CDSs)	31.1	11.9			
Other	0.3	0.1	1.7	0.4	37%
Equity-Linked Contracts	**6.9**	**6.8**	**0.8**	**0.5**	**<2%**
Commodity Contracts	**3.3**	**1.8**	**0.5**	**0.3**	
Gross Credit Exposure			**3.6**	**3.7**	

of default of their swap counterparty. Given that swap dealers are counterparties to practically all trades, the financial system is protected against the risk of contagion following the default of a dealer bank. Lastly, the financial system's transparency is enhanced since the majority of trades are booked with the CCP.

The post-crisis regulation has already exerted a profound impact on OTC derivative trading and on the management of credit risk by dealer banks. What long looked as an ineluctable increase in the volume and the credit risk of derivatives has been curved.

The total notional amount of outstanding OTC derivatives, the well-known emblematic statistic of the BIS, which has been exponentially increasing in the hundreds of trillion dollars, has peaked at $711 trillion in 2013 and then moved down to $493 trillion at the end-2015 (see Fig. 5). New capital, liquidity, and margining requirements have given dealers a strong incentive to reduce their swap books. Two dealers facing each other can net out a lot of positions and thus considerably reduce the number of derivative trades among them. This practice is called *trade compression*. They are helped by service providers such as the firm *TriOptima*, which run algorithms on derivative books and offer both parties to reduce their respective books while keeping the same market value and position.

Gross market value, which measures counterparty credit risk with the Mark-to-Market of the position, but before the application of bilateral netting agreements, and before collateral, has also gone down between end-June 2010 and end-June 2016 (from $24.7 to $20.7 trillion, see Table 2). Gross credit exposure, which reflects the impact of bilateral netting agreements, has stayed practically constant, going from $3.6 to $3.7 trillion.

3 A Still Uncomplete Reshaping

3.1 The Limitations of the New Framework

The Pittsburgh agenda had the clear ambition of addressing the complexity and the opacity of OTC derivative markets.

First, and in priority, through the centralization of clearing on CCPs, with the additional incentive of strengthened margining rules for uncleared derivatives. Second, and as imperatively, through the centralization of trading information on trade repositories (TRs). Third, and to the extent possible, through the very centralization of trading, on Swap Execution Facilities (SEFs).

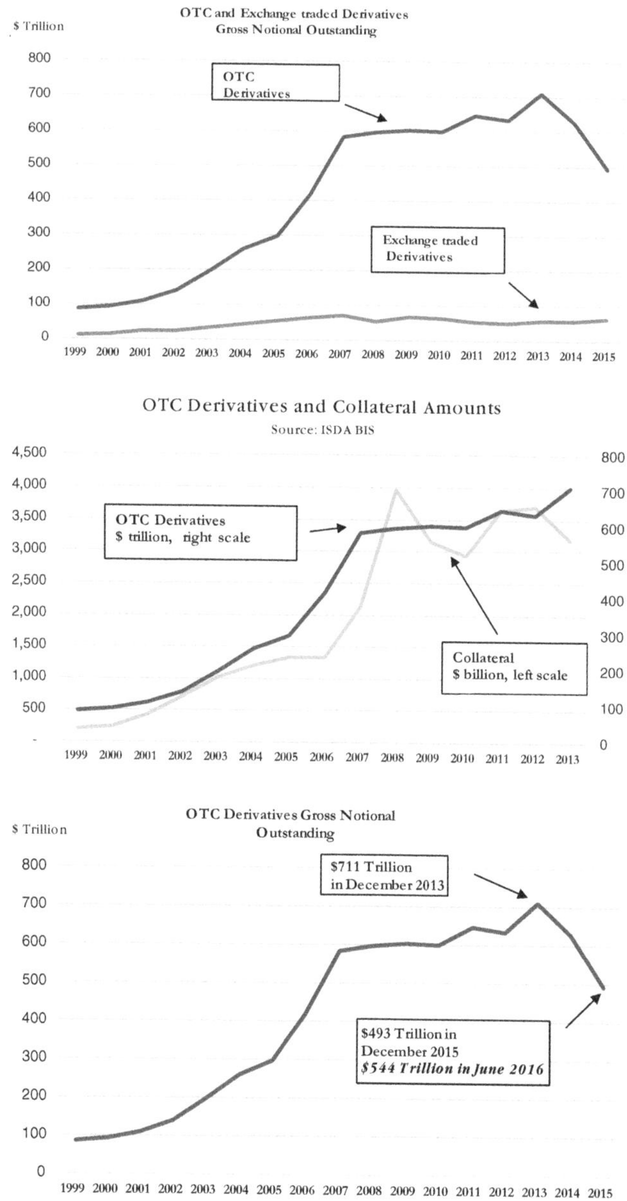

Fig. 5 Evolution of Total Notional Amount of Outstanding OTC Derivatives. *Source* BIS September 2016 Triennial Survey (Annual Data)

BIS OTC Derivatives Statistics at end-June 2016

At present, CCPs have become an essential focal point in derivatives markets. In Sect. 2.3, we saw how much of OTC derivative trading is now covered by CCPs, among which are well-established firms like LCH. Clearnet and CME, which are competing for the bulk of the clearing business.[5]

TRs have also been able to extend their data collection outreach. In a November 2015 report,[6] the FSB listed 27 TRs or TR-like entities worldwide, including DTCC, ICE, CME, and Unavista (the latter two being associated with and thus able to collect data from CME and LCH Clearnet).

Yet, although TRs can gather most of the information on OTC derivative trading in terms of post-trade data, the financial system (including regulators, analysts, or economists) seems unable to extract the full value of this extensive information. At this point therefore, one may say that the complexity of derivative markets trumps the comprehensiveness achieved in collecting trading data and makes full transparency a still distant if not elusive goal. In his June 2016 report presented at the ECB[7] in June 2016, the economist Darrell Duffie deplored the lack of a relevant framework to analyze trading collected in TRs, to organize them, and give them a meaning in a systemic risk preemption perspective.

Also, beyond the cognitive and analytical challenge, the FSB report points at the institutional obstacles to effective reporting: (i) the spreading of data across several jurisdictions for foreign exchange trades; (ii) the legal barriers to full access to data.

An example of such institutional barriers is the status given to FX swaps and FX forwards by the US Treasury in November 2012, exempting them from mandatory clearing and margin requirements.[8]

The area covered by the new regulation is also limited by the nature of market participants. For instance, under Dodd-Frank:

- a “Swap Dealer” (SD) and a “Major Swap Participant” (MSP) are subject to mandatory central clearing and to margining rules (with both initial and variation margin—see Chapter Restating the Role of Collateral on Collateral).
- But non-financial users are exempt: “*The final rules would establish initial and variation margin requirements for SDs and MSPs but would not require SDs and MSPs to collect margin from nonfinancial end users.*”[9]

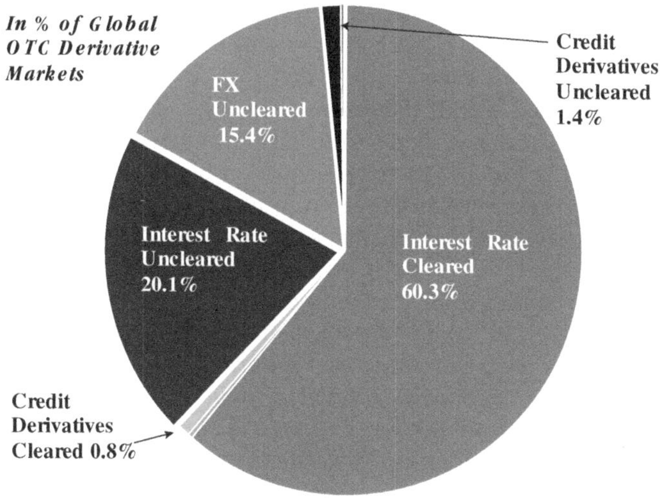

Fig. 6 Segments of Global OTC Derivative markets and percentages cleared on CCP or uncleared. *Source* BIS OTC Derivatives Statistics at end-June 2016

Lastly, derivatives trading has not moved in a meaningful way to trading platforms or SEFs. If use the area covered by CCPs as a simplifying indicator of the extension of the domain covered by the new post-2008 regulation (see Fig. 6), one finds about 40% of OTC derivatives trading still not in scope.

3.2 *The Unintended Consequences*

One has to examine post-2008 regulation in a holistic way, as part of a series of exceptional governmental actions taken to sustain the world economy through dire times. However decisive and specific they have been, none of the measures adopted for derivatives can be separated from the whole of the financial regulatory agenda, nor from the dominant role of monetary policy and the protracted period of low rates and abundant liquidity it has ushered to.

Having undergone a very severe shock, the global financial system had to go through a rigorous and comprehensive therapy. At the heart of such a radical treatment, there is always a trade-off: Priority has to be given to the patient's recovery, even if the cure implies a number of undesirable effects. Only if these effects remain contained can the treatment be considered a success.

In the post-2008 world, the trade-off may be expressed as: the priority is given to stronger, better capitalized, and less leveraged banks, even if it is at the expense of reduced market liquidity. At the heart of the trade-off is the strong incentive given to dealer banks, the nerves of global finance, to enhance their financial strength. In the words of the BIS, in June 2016:

Some outsize bond price movements point to changes in market liquidity, but lower leverage should support more robust liquidity under stress. At the same time, the persistence of low yields could worsen financial system weaknesses over the longer term, through a number of channels. Persistent market anomalies spread further. Examples included a widening of the cross-currency basis and negative US dollar interest rate swap spreads. These anomalies partly reflected market-specific supply-demand imbalances, sometimes reinforced by central bank actions. They also resulted from shifts in the behavior of large dealing institutions, which are now less active in arbitraging the anomalies away.

The post-2008 regulation had to preempt a new crisis by a proper and accurate translation, in capital and regulatory charges, of market, liquidity and leverage risks.

While OTC derivative markets were being reframed via central clearing and margining policies, international financial regulation was strengthening capital requirements that were deemed inadequate, and was introducing two ratios for liquidity risk and funding: the liquidity coverage ratio (LCR) and the net stable funding ratio (NSFR), plus a basic leverage ratio. The Basel Committee also launched a Fundamental Review of the Trading Book, to reinforce the regulatory capital regime of trading activities.

As dealer banks were seeing their trading costs increase, in particular the costs of ensuring strict compliance with the new rules, several among them opted for a significant reduction in their market making and trading activities. Some among them, like UBS, have decided to exit the trading business line and refocus on wealth management. A first consequence is that there are less market makers: The market is less liquid, less rigorously arbitraged, which gives way to anomalies such as the negative swap spreads in US dollar, seen since the last quarter of 2015 (see Fig. 7). Along with reduced secondary market liquidity, another direct

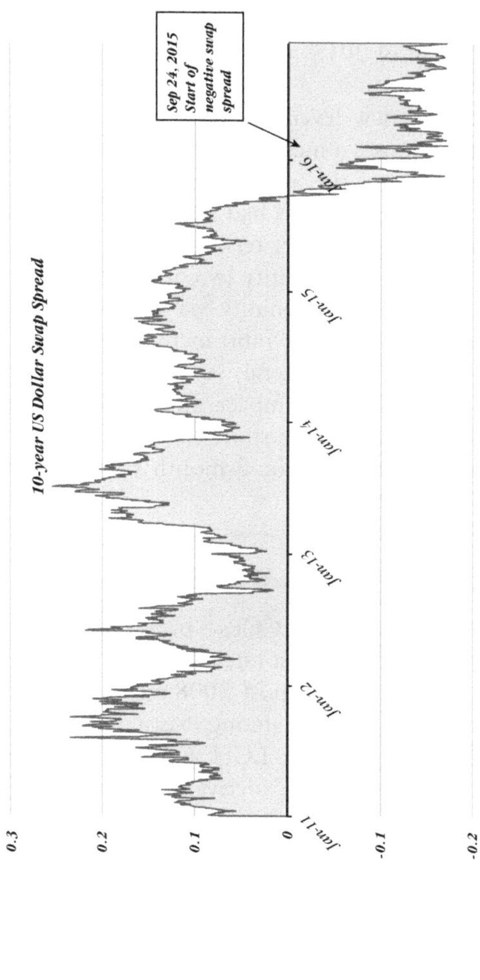

Fig. 7 The negative US Dollar Swap Spread since September 2015. *Source* Bloomberg, daily data, in %

consequence is that, with less active swap dealers, there is a higher concentration of counterparty credit risk on a small number of banks—for trades cleared outside of CCPs—or on a small number of CCPs for centrally cleared trades (see Sect. 3.3).

In general, dealer banks are less inclined to hold inventories of bonds. This means that an Asian central bank selling US Treasuries may have an immediate and strong impact on the level of US government rates, as was seen in the fall of 2015, when US Treasuries saw their rate move above swap rates.

The impact of the new leverage ratio has been widely studied. The new leverage ratio imposes a minimum level to the ratio capital to assets, irrespective of the risks of the assets. This minimum is set at 5% in the USA and at 3% in the EU. It has had a strong impact on repo markets, one of the main markets for short-term liquidity. Normally, dealer banks would provide liquidity to any entity by entering into a repo. The dealer bank would itself source the liquidity via another repo, while keeping a margin. However, the leverage ratio increases the cost of holding the Treasury bond received as collateral, so dealer banks have less appetite for repos. This has a disruptive impact. In the last quarter of 2015, the 3-month repo rate—the rate for short-term lending securitized by US government bonds—was above the 3-month Libor, a rate for unsecured interbank borrowing.

3.3 The New Systemic Threat

The centralization of clearing on CCPs—62% of all OTC derivatives outstanding and 80% of OTC interest rate swaps (see Sect. 2.3)—is probably the main accomplishment of the post-2008 reform.

Competition for market share among existing clearing houses have led to the emergence of two CCPs, LCH and CME, which are capturing almost all centrally cleared OTC derivative transactions. In December 2015, the *Financial Times* was reporting that the market share of CME was estimated by the specialized firm Clarus FT to be 30% while LCH. Clearnet was capturing most of the other 70%.

From an economic efficiency standpoint, this is a very favorable outcome: Large-sized CCPs can fully reap the benefits of netting transactions across a wide array of positions and are more likely to achieve natural hedges against the key risk to the CCP: The risk, after the default of a CCP counterparty, of a large change in its MtM, which would go much beyond the value of the collateral the CCP holds. Economists would tend to agree with the ideas formally demonstrated by the economists Darrell Duffie and Zhu in a 2011 article[10]: *counterparty credit risk in the OTC derivatives market is exacerbated by a multiplicity of CCPs,* and also: *counterparty risk is always reduced by merging the clearing activities of multiple CCPs into a single CCP.*

The problem is that CCPs have now become the new source of systemic risk, having grown into "too-big-to-fail" entities, comparable to SIFIs. Even worse, there is at present no regulatory framework for CCPs.

Prudential authorities have decided to use the tools that had been deployed to manage the systemic risk of SIFIs: first a framework for stress testing to help preempt any failure; then a resolution framework to help mitigate the impact of a failure.

In April 2015, the FSB, the Basel Committee, the Committee on Payments and Infrastructures (CPMI), and the International Organization of Securities Commissions (IOSCO), committed to a *joint work plan (…) to enhance resilience, recovery and resolvability of CCPs.* The key elements of the work plan included:

- Evaluation of resilience and loss absorption capacity through stress testing;
- Review of recovery mechanisms including loss allocation tools;
- Review of resolution regimes and resolution planning arrangements;
- Analysis of interconnections between CCPs and banks that are clearing members, analysis of channels for transmission of risk.

The European ESMA (European Securities Markets Agency) published the results of a first annual CCP stress test in April 2016 and assessed that the CCPs in the EU were showing resilience.

The policy discussion on how best to strengthen CCPs and avoid they become a new source of too-big-to-fail risk should continue in the coming years.

Notes

1. IMF, World Economic Outlook, Financial Stress, Downturns, and Recoveries, Executive Summary, October 2008 (IMF 2008).

2. Senate Committee on Banking, Housing, and Urban Affairs Chaired by Christopher J. Dodd: Questions for the Hearing on "Reducing Risks and Improving Oversight in the OTC Credit Derivatives Market" July 9, 2008 1 Questions for Dr. Darrell Duffie, Dean Witter Distinguished Professor of Finance, from Senator Crapo (Duffie and Hu 2008).
3. For reference, the other top priorities stated by the G20 Pittsburgh Meeting were: (i) Building high quality capital (for banks) and mitigating procyclicality; (ii) Reforming compensation practices to support financial stability; (iii) Addressing cross-border resolutions and systemically important financial institutions by end-2010.
4. Liquidity Coverage Ratio (LCR); Net Stable Funding Ratio (NSFR); Leverage Ratio.
5. At the time of this writing, in the second half of 2016, market participants could observe a "basis," a difference from 2 to 4 basis points, depending on maturities, in the rates quoted on interest rate swaps by dealers whether they would clear on CMD or on LCH.
6. FSB, Thematic Review on OTC Derivatives Trade Reporting, Peer Review Report, November 4, 2015 (FSB 2015).
7. Darrell Duffie, Financial Regulatory Reform after the Crisis: An Assessment, 2016 ECB Forum on Central Banking, June 2016 (Duffie 2016).
8. Note, however, that the US Treasury exemption does not apply to FX options, currency swaps and non-deliverable forwards.
9. CFTC Commodity Futures Trading Commission, January 6, 2016: *Margin Requirements for Uncleared Swaps for Swap Dealers and Major Swap Participants; Final Rule* (CFTC 2016).
10. Darrell Duffie and Haoxiang Zhu, *Does a Central Clearing Counterparty Reduce Counterparty Risk?* The Oxford University Press on behalf of the Society for Financial Studies, July 2011 (Duffie 2011).

References

BIS. (2016, November). *Statistical release, OTC derivatives statistics at end-June 2016, monetary and economic department.*

CFTC, Federal Register. (2016, January 6). *Margin requirements for uncleared swaps for swap dealers and major swap participants.* Vol. 81, No. 3.

Duffie, D. (2011). *On the clearing of foreign exchange derivatives*. Working Paper.

Duffie, D., & Hu H. (2008, June). *Competing for a share of global derivatives markets: Trends and policy choices for the US*. Stanford University WP 50.

Duffie, D. (2016, June). *Financial regulatory reform after the crisis: An assessment*. 2016 ECB Forum on Central Banking.

FSB. (2015, November). *Implementation and effects of the G20 financial regulatory reforms*. Report of the Financial Stability Board to G20 Leaders.

IMF. (2008, October). *Financial stress, downturns and recoveries*. World Economic Outlook. Washington DC: Intrenational Monetary Fund.

Outlining Counterparty Credit Risk Exposure

Abstract This chapter examines the very nature of Counterparty Credit Risk (CCR), or the manifestation of Credit and Default Risk in derivatives contracts, in which the exposure is measured at the level of a "Netting Set" of contracts, can change sign over time, and tends to be mitigated by the periodic posting of collateral. The chapter reviews how the growing awareness of CCR, considerably amplified by the 2008 crisis, has led to the entire revision of pricing methodologies for derivatives: inclusion of the Credit and Debt Value Adjustments, replacement of the Libor curve by the OIS curve (Overnight Index Swap) as the reference curve for discounting cash flows. The chapter then presents key metrics for measuring Counterparty Exposure and analyses the special case of Wrong-Way risk.

Keywords CCR counterparty credit rik · CDS credit default swap Collateral · CVA credit value adjustment · DVA debt value adjustment EE expected exposure · Effective EE (EPE) · EPE expected positive exposure · ISDA · Libor · No-Default value · Novation · OIS overnight interest swap · PFE potential future exposure · Wrong-way risk

I. Zelenko, *Credit Risk Management for Derivatives*,
DOI 10.1007/978-3-319-57975-7_2

1 Counterparty Credit Risk and OTC Derivatives

1.1 Definition: The Essence of Counterparty Credit Risk

Counterparty credit risk (CCR) is the form of Credit Risk that is specific to OTC derivatives. Several traits of OTC derivatives trading clearly distinguish CCR from traditional Credit Risk. Perhaps the main one is that, in a derivative contract (or in a portfolio of derivative contracts) among two parties, the sign of the exposure may vary over time. Let us examine the specifics of CCR by taking examples of standard cash and derivative products.

If A grants a 5-year $100 M loan to B, B owes a principal of $100 M to A plus a stream of interest over 5 years. All cash flows are known. A has exposure to B, and the exposure is well known over the lifetime of the loan. The potential default of B, its ability or willingness to pay, is the only unknown.

If instead, B has issued a 5-year $100 M marketable fixed rate bond purchased and held by A in the *Trading Portfolio* or the *Available for Sale Portfolio*, A is exposed to B for up to 5 years, and as long as A does not sell the bond. All future bond cash flows are known. While A has exposure on the market value of the bond (or Mark-to-Market or MtM), which may vary in many different and unpredictable ways over the 5 years, A has certainty about all future cash flows if A holds the bond to maturity: again the only unknown would be the potential default of B.

Let us now suppose that A enters into a 5-year $100 M notional fixed receiver interest rate swap with B (versus 6-month Libor) as in Figs. 1 and 2. The swap differs from the loan and from the bond in terms of both cash flows and exposure. The direction of net cash flows may change over the 5-year lifetime of the swap, going either from A to B or from B to A. The sign of the MtM, contrary to the case of the bond, may also change. This means, therefore, that the exposure may change sign over the life of the swap. The swap starts with zero value: In present value, the stream of fixed interest payments to A has initially the same present value as the stream of future Libor payments to B. The MtM may first be positive to A, and so A has exposure on B; but the MtM may then become negative to A, meaning that B is now exposed to A. Before the MtM eventually reverts back to zero, at the maturity of the swap, A and B may have alternatively the role of the creditor and that of the

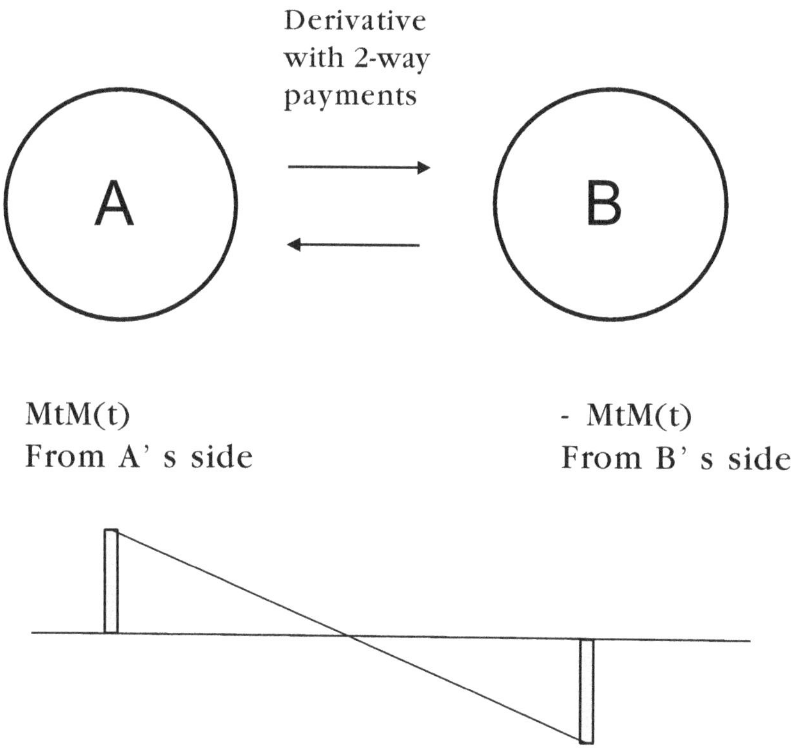

Fig. 1 Derivative with 2-way payments among counterparties

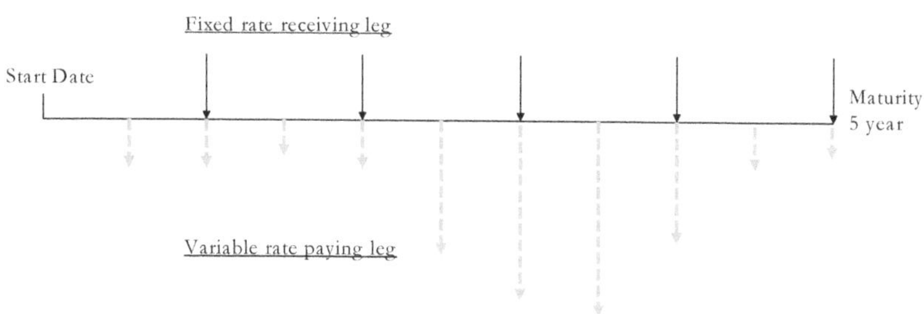

Fig. 2 Example of a 5-year Interest Rate Swap

debtor. And if the swap contract features collateral, A and B would be, alternatively, payer or receiver of collateral.

This mirror image of counterparties' roles, along with its uncertain dynamic, forms part of the essence of CCR.

Let us look at another example of derivative so as to highlight the bilateral nature of CCR: let us consider the purchase by A of a 1-year European call or put option sold by B. Once the premium is paid, the payment would only go from B to A. There may not be a payment if the option matures out of the money but if there is a payment it can only be from B to A. The MtM can end up with zero value but, over the lifetime of the option, the MtM will always be positive to A. A will always be exposed to B. In fact, several derivative market participants, who are wishing to limit risk, would restrict their derivative activity to the purchase of such call options. Yet, even in this simple case, there still is a substantial bilateral dimension. Assuming the call is collateralized, assuming no threshold (see Chap. "Restating the Role of Collateral" on Collateral), the flow of cash at inception will be: A pays the option premium to B, but then immediately receives the cash back from B in the form of collateral. Furthermore, if this purchase of a call option is cash neutral for A at inception, it may not remain the same over the lifetime of the option. If the option price were to go down after inception, A would have to pay back some of the collateral received and make cash payments to B.

In sum, portfolios of derivatives among two counterparties would, in general, lead to net values (MtMs) and payments which, unlike bonds, would go both ways.[1] See Figs. 1–3.

> CCR generally refers tothe bilateral credit risk of transactions with uncertain exposures that can vary over time with the movement of underlying market factors. (…) credit exposure depends on one or more underlying market factors. Instruments with CCR involve an exchange of payments or an exchange of a financial instrument against payment and are identified with an explicit counterparty for which a unique probability of default can be determined. CCR is bilateral; it exists for both parties to a transaction over the life of a contract. Other typical characteristics of transactions that involve CCR may include the use of collateral to mitigate risk[2];

The concept of CCR also applies to securitized financing transactions such as repos or reverse repos. A repo is a borrowing by a bank or a financial institution against the delivery of a security (generally a

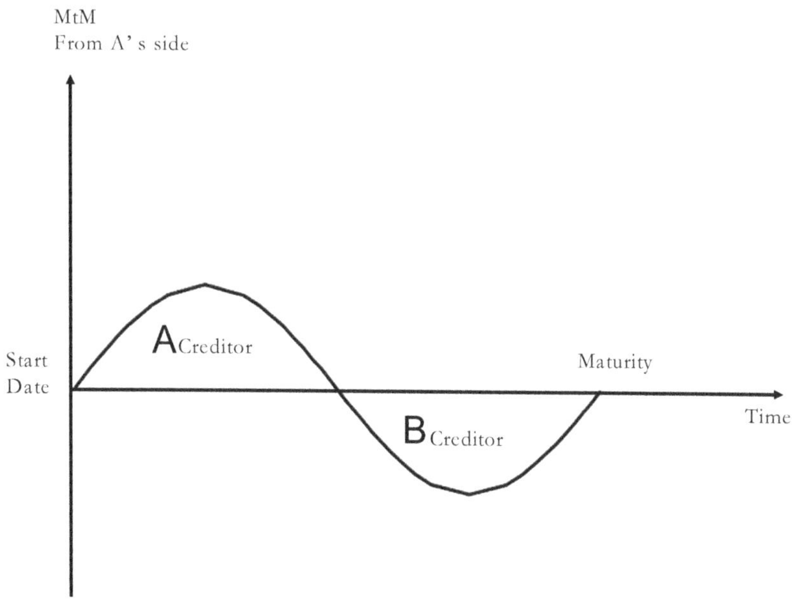

Fig. 3 Evolution of mark-to-market

government bond) which serves as collateral. We remain focused in what follows on OTC derivatives.

Due to the very nature of a derivative, its MtM may be determined by the price of other market instruments—the underlying variables in the case of options—and by the present and future values of interest rates used to discount cash flows. The uncertainty in the future values of variables driving the price of derivatives, be they simple interest rate swaps, or derivatives with embedded options (sometimes on a wide array of market instruments such as hybrids), will necessitate the use of Monte Carlo simulations.

Simulations will help capture the whole span of possible future paths for the MtM (see Fig. 4); in particular when embedded options create nonlinearity and path-dependent events. They will help compute the expected positive exposure taken over the life of the derivative.

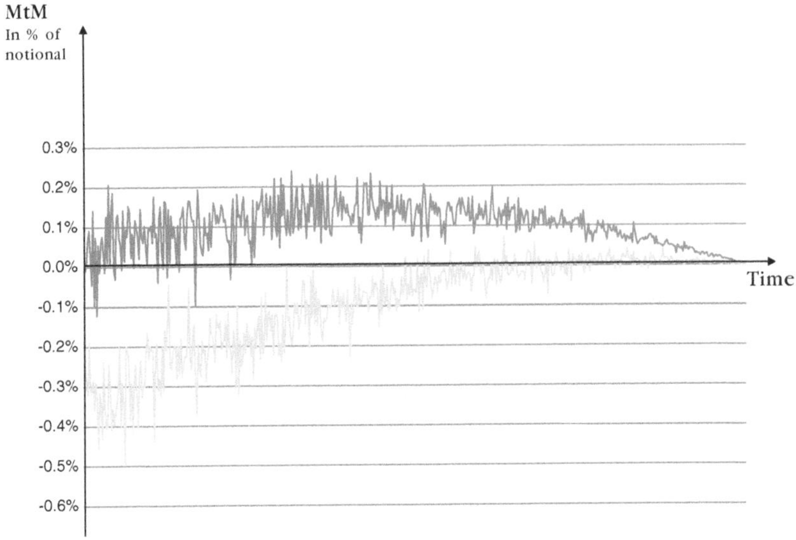

Fig. 4 MtM evolution of a 2-year zero-coupon swap under two rate scenarios

1.2 The Growing Recognition of Counterparty Credit Risk

Derivative markets are one of the hallmarks of modern finance; derivative transactions have been relentlessly growing in size since their appearance in the 1970s and up until the 2008 crisis, when the exponential growth suddenly stopped. Since then derivatives outstanding amounts have evolved in range then, since 2013 have been curbed down by the effects of regulation (see Fig. 5).

Derivatives have been answering a widespread need for managing the generalized volatility prevailing in rates, stock, foreign exchange, and commodity markets after the liberal reforms of banking and finance of the 1980s. Standardized or plain vanilla derivatives, such as futures or generic options, would be traded on exchanges. But most of the time, derivative end users would rather trade with a bank. Dealer banks offer them a wider and more straightforward access to all potential usages and sources of value offered by derivatives. Even more decisively, dealer banks would offer custom-tailored transactions adapted to the specific needs of their clients. Dealers would then share and hedge the risks of

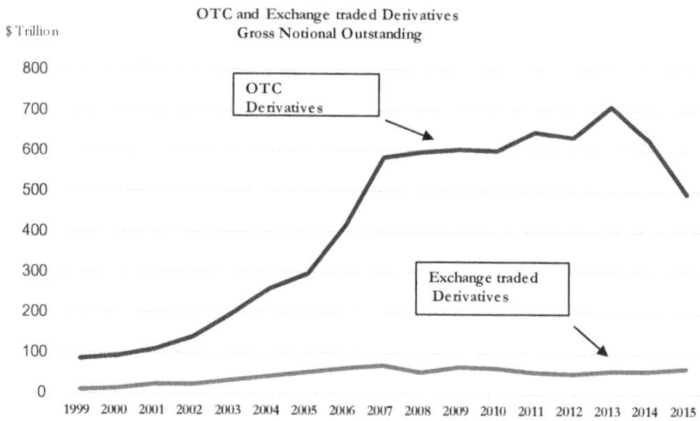

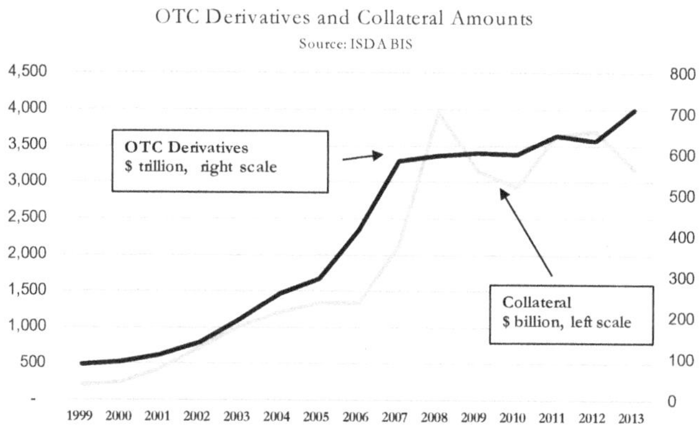

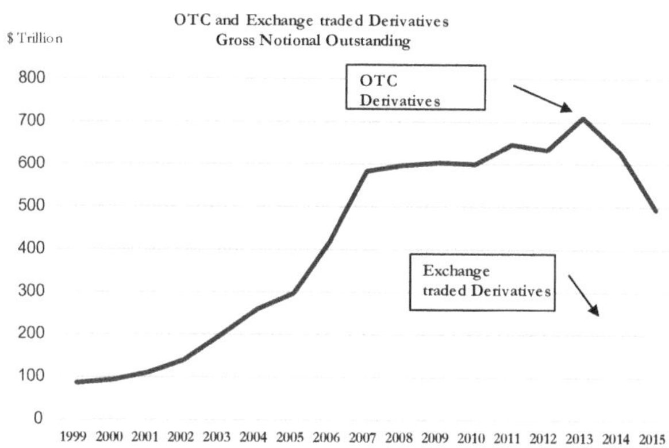

Fig. 5 OTC and Exchange Traded Derivatives outstanding amounts. *Source* BIS, in US Dollar Trillion

these bespoke transactions using simpler products, sparing their client such structuring and risk mitigation works. For these reasons, the bulk of the market has long been and continues to be in OTC derivatives (see Fig. 5), where transactions are "over-the-counter," among two counterparties, of which one would be a dealer bank.

In the 1980s and 1990s, derivatives have been wielding a tremendous market risk management power, creating a high degree of confidence in the ability to mitigate market risk. Initially, credit risk or default risk were momentarily relegated to the backdrop. Derivative pricing technology rapidly improved, developing a fairly sophisticated technology that would rely on highly abstract and arcane concepts such as the risk-neutral probability, which were nevertheless customarily used for valuation purpose. Risk-neutral probabilities, a cornerstone of derivative pricing, set probabilities on future values of market variables, derived from observed data, but adjusted to reflect the fact that those participating in the trading of derivatives should be risk neutral vis-a-vis market risk. This risk neutrality assumption reflects in turn the fundamental hypothesis that derivatives allow for the mitigation of all market risk present in the economy. Derivative markets are deemed to make markets *complete*, by providing a market for hedging every market risk.

But again, credit risk was initially an afterthought. In the market context of the 1980s and early 1990s, the pricing of derivatives totally abstracted from the risk of default. It was a time when fixed income markets were largely dominated by government bond trading, at least outside of the USA, and a time when banks were displaying a stronger credit quality than today or, rather, a time when a loss in derivatives trading was not likely to precipitate the failure of a bank. Quite characteristically, the practice of posting collateral had been introduced at this early stage, but the goal was then to protect the dealer bank against the default of a corporate user with a lower credit quality. Bank regulation in the 1980s, seeking to prevent bank failures, and as epitomized by the 1988 Basel Capital Accord, was primarily concerned with default risk in the lending book. Derivative trading was not narrowly associated with default, and the specifics of CCR were not fully understood nor outlined.

As corporate bond markets were becoming bigger in the 1990s, and as credit risk was starting to become a tradeable risk, with the appearance of credit derivatives, the methods for valuing default risk and CCR were added to finance textbooks and to the tool box of practitioners. In 1995, supervision authorities outlined the regulatory regime for CCR in the celebrated document: *Basel Capital Accord: Treatment of Potential Exposure for Off- Balance Sheet Items.*[3]

At the end 1990s and early 2000s, as the new Basel II Comprehensive Framework, inspired by an increased reliance on the self-regulation capacity of banks and markets, was being elaborated, specific preparation documents, published in 2005, outlined the key concepts and metrics for managing CCR. Among these concepts, which we will examine in more detail in this chapter, were the Potential Future Exposure (PFE), the Expected Exposure (EE), the Expected Positive Exposure (EPE), and the concept of Credit Value Adjustment (CVA), seen as the measure of the expected loss in the context of derivative transactions.

The development of all these new concepts had been actively led by quantitative analysts in investment banks and had been progressing extremely fast. In fact, by the time the Basel II Framework was published in 2006, a significant wave of concentration had happened in the banking sector, and notably among derivatives dealer banks, some of which owned a very sizeable market share, and a technological edge giving them a competitive advantage. Yet in 2006, derivatives were deployed to serve innovation and to push the frontier of capital markets, particularly in the domain of credit structured finance which proved fatal to the whole system. Credit risk metrics and credit valuation adjustments, reflecting an increasingly efficient CCR management, were geared toward improving pricing and reflecting all risks and transaction costs to clients.

The crisis of 2007–2008 and its aftermath gave a wholly different meaning and purpose to the implementation of the CCR technology. Governments were leading a full re-foundation of derivatives markets. Triggered by valuation and liquidity problems in credit derivatives markets, the crisis of 2007–2008, after the failure of Lehman Brothers, had resulted in an unprecedented paralysis of the global financial sphere, generating an extremely powerful negative shock on the global economy. When the Heads of State and Government gathered in 2009 in Pittsburg, under the aegis of the G20, with the objective to stabilize the financial system and to re-establish confidence, the twin questions of OTC derivatives markets and CCR were at the very top of the agenda. Accordingly, regulation made these questions a priority. At the September 2009 meeting in Pittsburgh, the G20 requested that all standardized derivatives be cleared on central clearing counterparties or CCPs. The new 2010 Basel Framework, Basel III, considerably reinforced the Basel II requirements for CCR, notably with the introduction of a new capital charge addressing the volatility of the CVA measure, and the implied risk for banks. In addition to Basel III, national regulators were strengthening the requirements for the collateralization (or the "margining") of derivatives transactions (see Chap. "Reshaping Derivatives Markets: The Post-2008 Ambition").

After 2008, governments had decided to establish new market structures and regulations to contain default risk in OTC derivative markets. The Basel III section on CCR starts with the statement:

Failure to capture major on- and off-balance sheet risks, as well as derivative related exposures, was a key factor that amplified the crisis

2 Credit Risk in Derivative Pricing

The theory of derivative pricing, implemented and perfected over time by derivatives markets and the dealer banks' industry, rests on a few fundamental principles:

- The price of an instrument should reflect its risk;
- The price should reflect risk but not risk aversion; the price is the expectation of the present value of all future cash flows, computed with a risk-neutral probability expressing the assumption that there should not be risk aversion in derivative markets, since they are *complete* and thus allow for the hedging of all risks;
- Future cash flows are discounted at the *risk-free rate* to obtain a *no-default valuation*. The credit risk of the parties to a transaction are computed separately as Credit Value Adjustment (CVA) and Debt Value Adjustment (DVA), and added to the *no-default price* (see Chap. "Adjusting for Credit and Debt Value: CVA and DVA" on CVA and DVA).

$$V = V_{ND} + CVA + DVA$$
$$V_{ND} : \text{No-default price} \qquad (1)$$

This chapter deals with the *no-default price* estimate and how the definition and the estimation of a risk-free yield curve has evolved since the 2008 crisis.

The agreement on a risk-free yield curve, reliable and easily computable from observed market data, and on the risk-free discount factors that can be derived from it is of course essential to the calculation of any derivative's *no-default price*.

2.1 The Long Reliance on Libor as a Risk-Free Rate Proxy

The most widely traded derivative has been and continues to be the interest rate swap (IRS), in which a fixed rate and a Libor rate coupon, computed on the same notional, are periodically exchanged among two counterparties. The largest IRS market is the dollar IRS market, in which the standard is to exchange payments every 3 month, with the floating rate coupon referenced on the value of the Libor 3-month taken at the beginning of the period.

In the 1980s, the choice of the Libor as a proxy for the risk-free interest rate was a natural choice for swap dealers. The present value (PV) of the Libor leg would be always close to par (being exactly par at the reset of the Libor). Moreover, because of the strong credit quality of the banks, Libor rates would never be too far from government rates (Treasury Bills in the USA) of the same maturity.

Libor rates provide indications of unsecured rates in the interbank market for overnight and 1-, 3-, 6-, and 12-month borrowings. Libor rates are obtained on every business days by polling a panel of selected banks. The fact that Libor values are obtained from polling banks and do not directly from the rates observed in transactions has been much discussed in the aftermath of the 2008 crisis, as the representativeness of Libor values, with regard to liquidity conditions and to the creditworthiness of banks, became intensely disputed. Yet before 2007–2008, and for quite a long time, the values of the Libor rates published in all major currencies by the British Bankers Association (BBA) were seen as reliable indicators of borrowing costs of the interbank market. Interbank lending and borrowing operations in all main currencies were taking place in London in "Euro markets" or international or "offshore" markets (Eurodollar, Euroyen, Eurodeutschemark, etc.). But, while rates were not directly observable in these Euro markets; Libor values were reliable and more convenient to use. Therefore, Libor became the main reference, and the Libor curve (Libor rates up to one year, swap rates from 2 to 30 years) the source of risk-free discount factors for pricing swaps and other derivatives.

When generating the Libor-swap yield curve (or "bootstrapping") from a number of observed values, banks would use Eurodollar futures to generate the short end of the curve, would then use Libor rates, and, beyond one year, would turn to swap rates quoted by brokers.

2.2 *The Deficiencies of the Libor Rate After 2008*

During the 2007–2008 crisis, the sudden and protracted disappearance of liquidity in the interbank market, with the paralysis, and the cessation of lending and borrowing transactions, constituted perhaps the highest cause of concern for the viability of the entire financial system. The shortcomings of Libor as a risk-free rate proxy were then starkly exposed. In the aftermath of 2008, and in the Euro sovereign crisis that followed, the shortcomings of the Libor have been considered as structural enough to inspire the industry discontinuing the use of the Libor.

By contrast, during the prior systemic financial crisis, the 1997–1998 Asian crisis, the Libor curve had proven to constitute a stable reference for pricing credit risk, and soon after the crisis, the majority of bonds issued in global financial markets were priced relative to the Libor curve.

But in the 2007–2008 crisis, rather than stability and continuity, Libor rates inspired suspicion and unreliability. Libor rates, as evidenced by glaring price abnormalities, were failing to properly reflect the rapidly evolving dynamics in cash and derivatives interbank markets. The main weaknesses of their institutional design and underlying governance became all of a sudden very evident. Libor was overly reliant on the interbank unsecured borrowing market. Yet the crisis had shown that this market could cease to function, with liquidity and transactions migrating elsewhere. The abnormal Libor values also pointed to the fact that the Libor fixing, rather than an observed market price, was the outcome of a consultation process, which was vulnerable to manipulation and rigging (see Box 1).

Looking at the evolution of Libor rates, one can get a more concrete idea of the high degree of instability and anomaly which characterized Libor rates in the 2007–2008 crisis and in the 2010 European bank-sovereign crisis.

Box 1: The 2012 Libor Scandal: A Foundation of Finance Shaken to its Roots

The Libor or London Inter Bank Offered Rate was introduced in the eighties as trading in interest rate derivatives, and particularly in fixed for floating Interest Rate Swaps (IRS) was rapidly growing. There was a pressing need to standardize market practice, to establish a single definition, formalize a procedure, and governance for estimating and publishing, on every business day, the interbank short-term borrowing rate referenced as the floating rate in most derivatives contracts.

The British Bankers Association (BBA) answered this need. In 1986, the BBA started to coordinate the calculations of Libor fixings for the US dollar the Japanese yen and the British pound. The Libor fixing has since been published on each business day at 11:30a.m. GMT in London. The Libor fixing process consists in a survey. A panel comprised of 16 large and creditworthy banks operating in London (18 banks for the dollar Libor) are asked the question: *"At what rate could you borrow funds, were you to do so by asking for and then accepting interbank offers in a reasonable market size just prior to 11am?"*. Banks from the panel would send their predictions to the firm *Thomson Reuters*, which would calculate the average, having excluded the highest and lowest 25%, and would then publish the Libor fixing on behalf of the BBA. In 2012, there were Libor fixings for 10 currencies, with 15 maturity terms, ranging from overnight to 1 year. An estimated $300 trillion in of swap and future contracts were using Libor as the primary reference rate.

However, in 2012 an investigation revealed that several banks, among which Deutsche Bank, Barclays, UBS, Rabobank, and the Royal Bank of Scotland had been involved in rigging the Libor fixing for profit. Allegedly, several panel banks had underreported their borrowing costs by significant amounts with the intention to signal their financial strength at a time of market stress. Also, banks were alleged to have manipulated the fixing in order to generate gains in Libor-based derivatives. In 2012, the investigation led to the resignations of the CEOs of Barclays and Rabobank.

The Chancellor of the Exchequer published the Wheatley Review of LIBOR in September 2012. The review proposed to exclude illiquid segments of the interbank markets, where trading and liquidity would be too shallow to justify an indication. The Wheatley review also proposed that rates observed in transactions be incorporated in the estimate process, also to reduce the incentive to underreport funding costs to convey an image of financial strength: *"The BBA should publish individual LIBOR submissions after three months to reduce the potential for submitters to attempt manipulation, and to reduce and potential interpretation of submissions as a signal of creditworthiness."*

In 2013, the Financial Services Authority (FSA) acted and moved the supervision of the Libor from the BBA to the ICE

Benchmark Administration Ltd, an entity of the Intercontinental Exchange Group (ICE) regulated by the FSA. The FSA also implemented the recommendation of the Wheatley review: ICE was asked to anchor its calculation on transactions data; individual LIBOR submissions from banks would no longer be immediately viewable. Monitoring by regulators of traders' activity was also reinforced and criminal sanctions were introduced for rate manipulation.

Investigations continued and involved other major institutions. By May 2015, regulators in the USA, the UK, and the EU had fined banks more than $9 billion for rigging Libor. Sixteen banks were still exposed to the risk of lawsuits for an estimated total $35 billion. Large banks have prohibited the use of online "chat rooms" as an additional prevention against collusive behavior.

Instability in Libor and interbank markets can be found in the time series of the dollar Libor 3-month relative to the dollar 3-month Treasury bill rate (see Fig. 6). This spread, the *Ted spread*, might have revealed the sudden flight to quality that characterizes fear in times of market stress and/or crisis: in that sense, the Libor rate might have been considered as stable while the sudden run for US government paper would make government rates abnormally low for a short period of time. But at the same time, Libor rates in dollar were also no longer moving in sync with key rates, the Fed Funds and the OIS rates, which were directly connected to the liquidity on the interbank market (see Fig. 7).

The disruption in interbank markets became also particularly visible in Libor currency basis swap spreads. Spreads versus Libor in currency basis swaps are still not reflecting well-functioning markets (see Chap. "Reshaping Derivatives MarketsThe Post-2008 Ambition").

The currency basis swap is a convenient way for a bank or any market participant to convert a floating rate debt denominated in a currency—for instance a dollar debt on which the USD Libor is paid every 3 months—into a floating rate debt denominated in another currency and referenced on this currency's Libor or its equivalent—for instance a euro debt with a 3-month Euribor coupon.

A short-term basis swap, with a 3-month, 6-month or 1-year maturity, replicates the following cash borrowing and lending operations

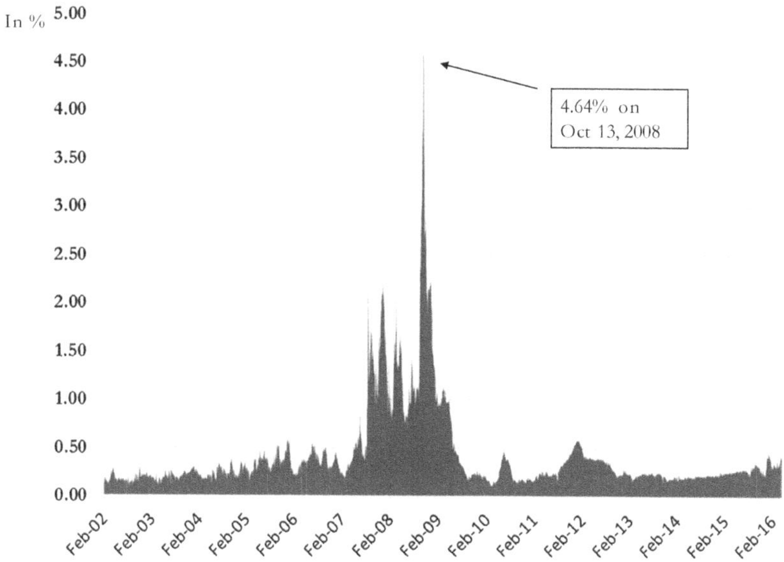

Fig. 6 USD libor 3-month minus Generic US Treasury Bill 3-month daily data February 1, 2002–April 8, 2016. *Source* Bloomberg

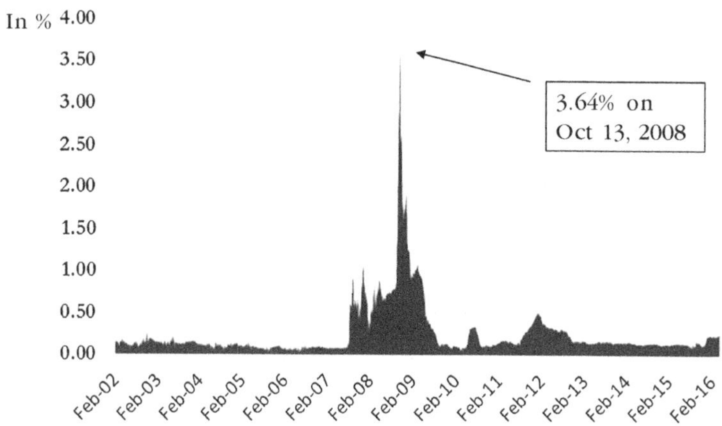

Fig. 7 USD libor 3-month minus USD OIS 3-month rate daily data February 1, 2002–April 8, 2016. *Source* Bloomberg

(in the case of a 6-month basis swap) among two banks (assuming 1 EUR = 1.10 USD at inception).

- Bank A lends USD110M to Bank B over 6 months and receives at maturity USD110M + USD Libor 6m.
- Bank B lends EUR100M to Bank A and receives at the 6m maturity EUR100M + Euribor 6m plus spread.

One can see that if Bank A and Bank B are banks with the average credit quality of banks in the Libor and Euribor panels, the spread should be very small. Otherwise, if interbank and FX markets function normally, any bank could replicate the basis swap in the cash and FX markets and gain from a risk-free arbitrage.

In basis swap markets, the market convention is that USD leg always pays or receives USD Libor, while the other leg is quoted as JPY Libor plus a spread or Euribor plus a spread.

Effectively, up to the summer of 2007 when the crisis began, basis swap spreads were customarily in the order of a few basis points and less than 5 basis points.

But starting in August 2007, the spreads relative to the Libor and Euribor indexes reached values that were no longer aligned with the no-arbitrage pricing theory. Spreads were rather showing the stress endured by the financial system and the insufficient liquidity in interbank markets. In 2007, European banks were experiencing difficulties in obtaining short-term dollar funding at Libor. They attempted to obtain dollars through the basis swap market. The EUR/USD basis swap spread moved away from its usual 5 basis points range around 0 to reach values as high as 126 basis points that were simply reflecting a major imbalance between supply and demand a major market disequilibrium. This lasted until the ECB offered dollar lines to European banks. But even then, the 3-month EUR/USD basis swap stabilized at levels around 50 basis points. The same move away from equilibrium happened again when the European sovereign crisis in 2010 (Fig. 8). The ongoing high levels at present could result from the reduced appetite of dealer banks to arbitrage abnormal values because of the capital requirements of the post-2008 regulation (see Chap. "Reshaping Derivatives MarketsThe Post-2008 Ambition").

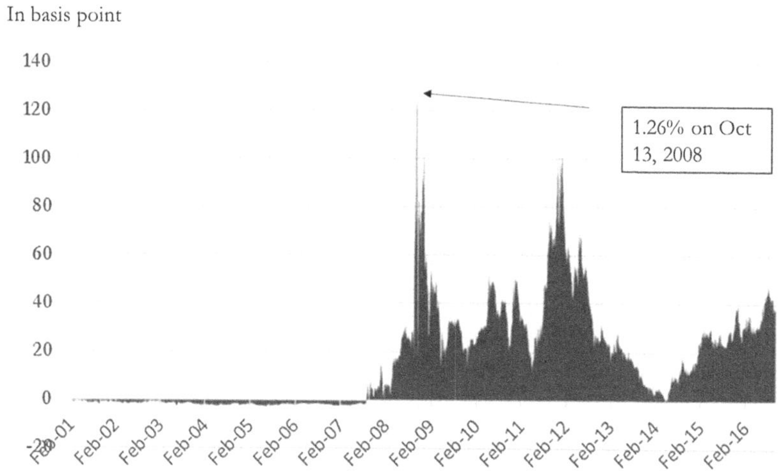

Fig. 8 EUR USD basis swap spread February 1, 2001 September 28, 2016 daily data. *Source* Bloomberg

The limitations of the Libor inspired the search for another and more reliable risk-free curve.

2.3 *The New Risk-Free Rate for Pricing Derivatives: The OIS*

The OIS rate is the Overnight Interest Swap rate. The dollar OIS is the rate for a swap against the overnight Federal Funds rate (Fed Funds), usually of a short maturity—up to 3 months. For example, in a 3-month dollar OIS swap, one of the parties—the fixed leg payer—pays, at the end of the 3-month period, a fixed rate on a given notional, while the other party (floating leg payer) pays, on the same notional, an interest compounded daily at the Fed Funds rate. There are now longer tenors for OIS swaps, going beyond 1 year. In a 5-year OIS swap, there would be quarterly or semi-annual payments computed as in the 3-month OIS.

The dollar OIS rate has a close relation with the Fed Funds market. One can see the floating leg payment of the OIS as the interest gained by rolling over a loan at the Fed Funds rate.

Let us now go over the rationale for electing the OIS as the new risk-free rate for the valuation of swaps and other derivatives.

The OIS rate is the rate of a swap against the overnight Fed Funds rate. In the OIS swap rate, there are two distinct elements of credit risk:

- The credit risk present in the overnight Federal Funds rate;
- The CCR present in the OIS swap itself.

The Fed Funds market is the interbank market for unsecured overnight borrowing in US dollars among US banks. In this market, transactions are executed through brokers. Every day, Fed Funds brokers will report to the Federal Reserve Bank of New York the average, weighted by amounts, of rates agreed among counterparts in all transactions. This average is called the *Effective Federal Funds rate* or *Effective Fed Funds* rate. This Effective Fed Funds rate is the rate that is compounded daily in the dollar OIS swap. In the euro market, the equivalent to the Effective Fed Funds is the EONIA (Euro Overnight Index Average). In the British Pound market, it is the SONIA (Sterling Overnight Index Average).

The overnight Fed Funds contains the average credit spread on banks operating in the USA.

The Repo—or repurchase agreement—is a money market transaction which is collateralized. The overnight repo rate where the collateral consists of US Treasury bonds is the risk-free comparator to the Fed Funds in overnight borrowing.

In a 2013 study on OIS and Libor rates,[5] J. Hull and A. White reported that before the start of the crisis and up to mid-2007, rates on overnight repos secured by the US government paper were 5–10 basis points below the Effective Fed Funds, and that, during the crisis, rates on repos secured by the US government fell relative to Fed Funds. Hull and White also estimated that over 2009–2012:

- The spread of Effective Fed Funds rate to a risk-free rate obtained by extrapolating short-term T-Bills was about 5 basis points.
- The overnight Libor rate was on average 6 basis points above the Effective Fed Funds.
- The overnight Libor rate was therefore 11 basis points above the overnight risk-free rate.

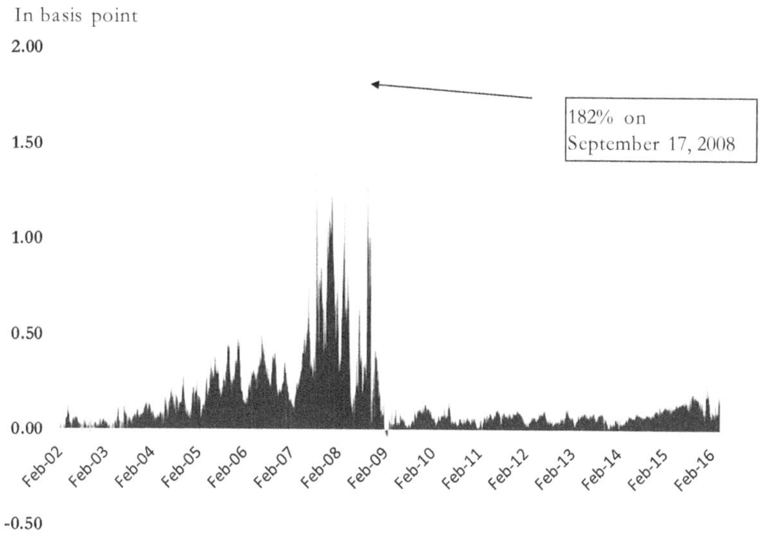

Fig. 9 USD OIS 3-month versus 3-month USD T-bill daily data February 1, 2002–April 8, 2016. *Source* Bloomberg

Let us now look at the OIS versus the T-bill rate at the 3-month horizon (see Fig. 9).

The OIS rate incorporates CCR. But the interdealer OIS swaps are fully collateralized. Moreover, for small maturities of 3 months or 6 months, and with bank counterparties of the same credit quality, the bilateral CVA adjustment, if reflected in the swap rate, should remain *de minimis.*

Using daily data from Bloomberg, we find that the average spread between the OIS and the T-bill at the 3-month horizon has been 16 basis points between February 2002 and April 2016 (a period which covers the 2008 and the European sovereign crises). This average spread moves down to 8 basis points between March 2012 and April 2016. One can also see from the curve that trading levels of the 3-month OIS, while they fully reflected the stress in the interbank market for short-term funds in 2008, rapidly stabilized once corrective actions were taken, and then durably reverted back within a 25 basis point range early in 2009.

At the same time, the average spreads between Libor and the T-bill at the 3-month horizon, taken over the same periods as above, have been, respectively, 42 basis points and 27 basis points.

Based on the arguments and data above, one can appreciate the rationale for choosing the OIS as both a reliable and a practicable proxy for the risk-free rate.

3 Counterparty Credit Risk Exposure Metrics

In this section, we will use the risk taxonomy adopted by regulation, the derivatives industry, within the International Swap Dealer Association (ISDA) and by the financial reporting rule-making bodies, notably expressed in the International Financial Reporting Standards (IFRS). These metrics have been set forth in consultation with market participants.

3.1 Measure at Portfolio Level: Netting Set

The first key concept is that of *Netting Set*. An OTC Derivative is governed by a contract using rules agreed among market participants in the ISDA forum. The ISDA contract among two counterparties defines all aspects pertaining to CCR and the possibility of default by one of the parties. The ISDA contract applies to a *Netting Set*, the set of transactions that have been concluded with reference to and under the agreed provisions of the ISDA contact. The ISDA contract is legally enforceable.

The term *Netting* specifically refers to the fact that the first key measure for counterparty risk, the MtM, defining the value of the contract, the exposure, the exposure at default, and the claim for the surviving entity is going to be calculated as one aggregated position whose individual values can offset or net the values of other individual instruments in the portfolio.

3.2 Key Aspects of Counterparty Risk Exposure Metrics

3.2.1 Rest on Future MtM Probability Distributions and Simulations

There are a number of key metrics, which all recognize the uncertainty embedded in derivatives and measure CCR exposure based on the MtM probability distribution at future points in time or, instead, based on the simulations of a large number of paths (in millions) the MtM of the portfolio could follow until the maturity of the instrument with the longest tenor.

3.2.2 Define Exposure as per the ISDA Contract and Reflect Collateral

Exposure is always measured by applying the terms of the ISDA contract to the MtM computed on the Netting Set. In what follows, we will start by describing exposure metrics without any consideration for collateral. In practice, however, most ISDA contracts include collateral nowadays. Including the effect of collateral in measuring future exposure makes calculations more challenging.

3.2.3 Focus on Positive Exposure Only

Exposure metrics solve the problem of the 2-way nature of CCR by considering only the positive side of the exposure, or by focusing in algebraic terms on:

$$Max(MtM; 0)$$

In the chapter on CVA, with the importance of the DVA measure, and also with the importance of credit risk on posted collateral, we will use "negative metrics" that play the symmetric role of the "positive metrics" for exposure.

3.2.4 Reflect the "Time Element" of Derivative's Exposure

Contrary to standard measures of Market Risk or Credit Risk on portfolio instruments, CCR metrics cover the derivative portfolio over its entire life, until the maturity of the longest tenor instrument. One of the reasons for this is that OTC derivatives are contracts that are not meant to be traded on a secondary market and prove rather difficult to dispose of before maturity: they are difficult to terminate before maturity (an agreement has to be reached with the counterparty) and difficult to "re-assign" or "novate", which is to be replaced by another counterparty (an agreement has to be reached among three banks). The prudent approach of CCR is to consider that all derivatives in the portfolio will remain on the books of the entity measuring its risk until they mature.

Another aspect of time is the "rollover" of shorter dated derivatives. Certain derivatives in the portfolio may have an exposure that peaks in the medium term, say in three years; however, this exposure, measured at the 3-year horizon may not be the right measure of the maximum

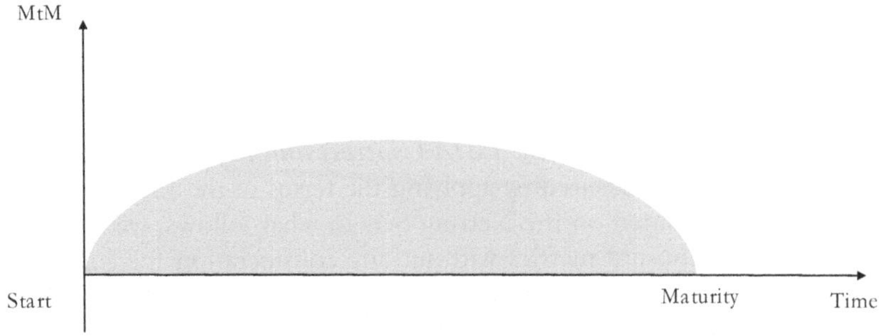

Fig. 10 Typical Counterparty Credit Risk Exposure for an Interest Rate Swap (IRS)

exposure over the life of the portfolio, as shorter term derivative with a peak exposure in the coming 6 months will be rolled over at the identical and add to the total exposure in 3 years. The prudent exposure metric should aggregate those two exposures. This is the logic governing the *Effective Expected Exposure* indicator.

3.3 Basic Intuitions on Swap Credit Exposure

Bankers would generally characterize credit risk of interest rate swaps (IRS) and currency swaps (CS) with the two following illustrations. Since these swaps still form the majority of OTC derivatives portfolios having these shapes in mind also helps grasping the intuition of CCR in a portfolio. The IRS would normally start with zero MtM. The fixed rate receiving party may see the value increase if the swap curve moves down during the life of the swap, in line with the duration of the fixed leg, like a bond; as maturity approaches, however, the value of the fixed leg reverts back to par and the swap MtM converges toward zero (see Fig. 10). A CS, on the other hand, may end up with a positive value. The CS starts with the initial exchange of the two currencies at the then prevailing rate. The initial exchange has to be performed in reverse on maturity date and may have value at this time if the receiving currency has appreciated after start date (see Fig. 11).

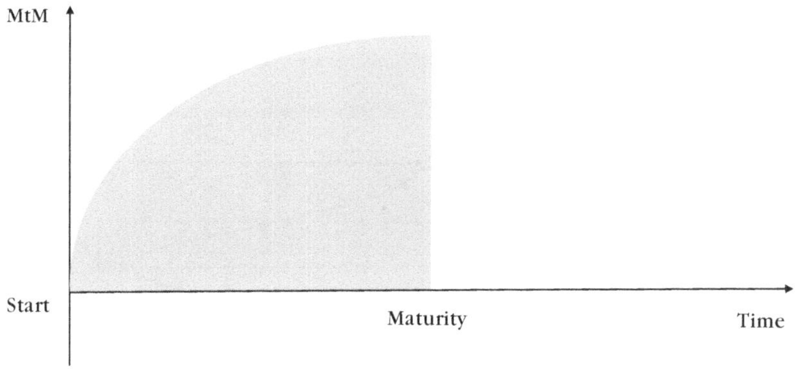

Fig. 11 Typical Counterparty Credit Risk Exposure for a Currency Swap (CS)

3.4 Main Counterparty Credit Risk Exposure Metrics

At a future point in time: Expected Exposure (EE) and Potential Future Exposure (PFE)

The two basic metrics, EE and PFE, characterize the distribution of the positive MtM at a future point in time: EE is the expectation of this distribution; the PFE is the 99% maximum increase in MtM until the future date considered (see Fig. 12).

Both EE and PFE would be generated by the same Monte Carlo risk model which simulates all possible paths (say 5 million paths for the MtM of the derivative portfolio or Netting Set—until the final maturity of the instrument with the longest tenor). At a future point in time, EE is the average value of all positive values of the Monte Carlo simulation; PFE is the 99% quantile of the distribution of positive values.

Figure 12 shows the MtM at time t and the distribution of all MtM possible paths at time $t + \Delta t$ with EE and PFE being the expectation and the 99% quantile of all positive values, respectively.

3.4.1 Over the Entire Portfolio's Life: Expected Positive Exposure (EPE), Effective EPE

There is one EE and one PFE defined for each time in the future. We now look at metrics with encompassing the evolution of CCR exposure over the entire life of the portfolio (see Fig. 13).

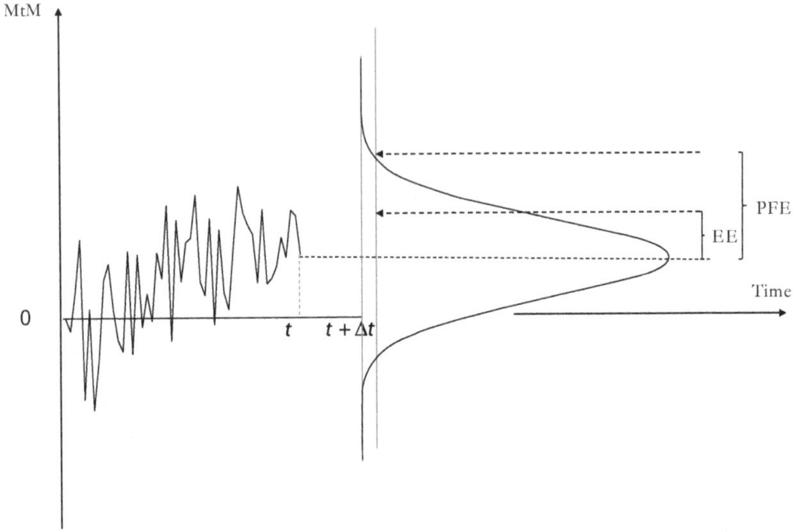

Fig. 12 EE and PFE at a future time *t*

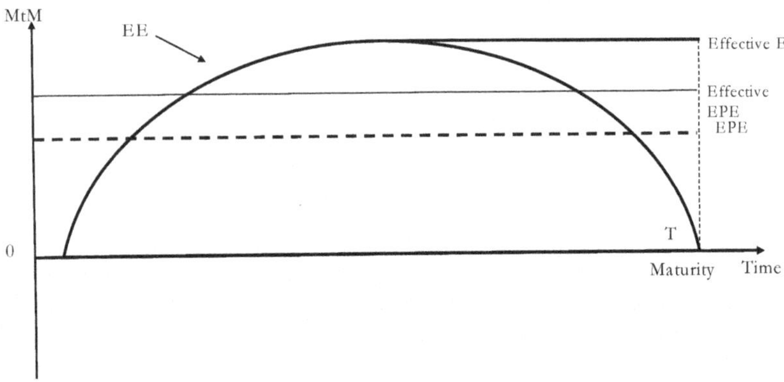

Fig. 13 EE. EPE, Effective EE and Effective EPE

The *Expected Positive Exposure* is the time-weighted average of EE estimated for a mapping of all future time horizons.

We saw that one of the potential flaws of exposure modeling was residing in the rolling over of derivatives position with short maturities: the rollover might be aggregated with a peak exposure at a future point in the future and produce an "accumulation of exposure" that could not be captured with point-in-time measures.

This is the rationale for defining the Effective EE and the Effective Expected Positive Exposure.

Effective Expected Exposure (*Effective EE*) is defined in a recursive manner by increasing, point by point, the time horizon and taking the maximum of: the Effective EE obtained until then, and the EE computed for the next point. In algebraic terms this gives:

For all t_k $k = 1 \ldots N$ and t_N being the final maturity of the Netting Set:

$$EffectiveEE(t_k) = Max[Effective\,EE(t_{k-1}); EE(t_k)] \tag{2}$$

The *Effective Expected Positive Exposure* is the time-weighted average of *Effective Expected Exposures* taken over all the dates mapping the forecasting horizon until the final maturity of the *Netting Set*.

4 Wrong-Way Risk

Wrong-way risk can be defined as the concomitant increase of the following:

- The credit exposure to a counterparty;
- The credit weakness of this counterparty.

In bond markets, the increase in the perceived credit weakness of the issuer of the bond would translate in an increase in the bond's credit spread, therefore a reduction in the bond market price, which also measures the instantaneous exposure on the issuer. Counterparty's credit quality and counterparty exposure move in opposite directions: this is the usual "Right-way risk."

Wrong-way risk exhibits the opposite property: the credit weakness of the counterparty and the credit exposure on the counterparty increase at the same time.

Wrong-way risk finds its source in the correlation between the exposure to a counterparty and the probability of that counterparty defaulting. One may first think that, at the margin, this is simply a logical consequence of an OTC derivative: if the MtM becomes positive for A and negative for B, the exposure of A increases while, at the same time, B's financial strength is marginally altered by its negative MtM. But in a normal situation, this incremental effect would not, in itself, lead to Wrong-way risk as it is only a marginal deterioration in the financial position of B, which may also have other positions in its balance sheet offsetting this single loss. One speaks of Wrong-way risk when the negative link between exposure and credit strength is both structural and substantive.

Wrong-way Risk, sometimes also called Wrong-way exposure, had been identified as a concern as early as the end 1990s[6] and had been included in the long preparation phase of Basel II, becoming part of the dialogue between regulators and the banking industry. But it is really after the 2008 crisis that Wrong-way risk entered more forcefully the list of CCR concepts and metrics, and became fully endorsed by both market participants and regulators. Because Wrong-way risk had materialized in a significant way and had manifested itself as a key vulnerability of the financial system.

In working with the Basel Committee on regulatory capital for CCR, in 2001, the ISDA defined Wrong-way risk as[7]:

> Wrong-way risk occurs when exposure to a counterparty is adversely correlated with the credit quality of that counterparty. Wrong-way risk, as an additional source of risk, is rightly of concern to banks and regulators.

The 2006 Basel II reference document defines *General Wrong-way risk* and *Specific Wrong-way risk* as "CCR-related risks" as:

General Wrong-Way Risk *arises when the probability of default of counterparties is positively correlated with general market risk factors.*

Specific Wrong-Way Risk *arises when the exposure to a particular counterpart is positively correlated with the probability of default of the counterparty due to the nature of the transactions with the counterparty.*

4.1 Wrong-Way Risk in Practice

Wrong-way risk arises in a number of typical trading situations.

Credit Derivatives Credit derivatives are more prone to generate Wrong-way risk by their nature. Figure 14 below outlines the causality chain

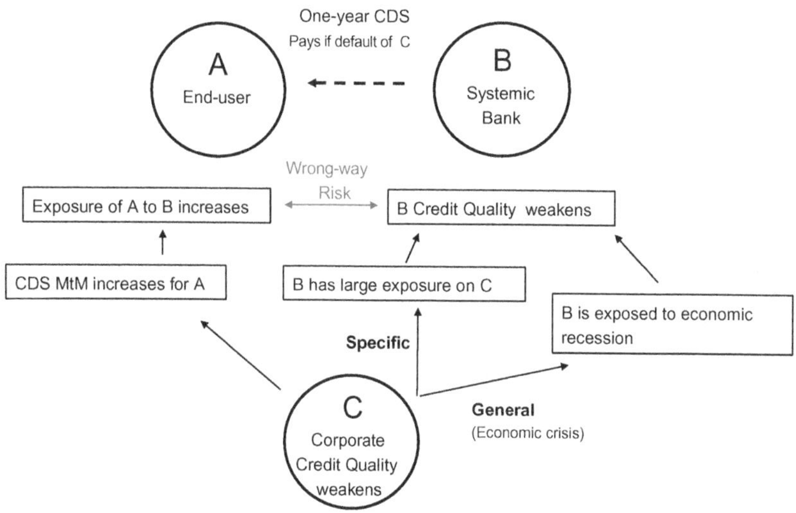

Fig. 14 Wrong-way risk in a Credit Default Swap (CDS)

between credit quality and credit exposure. In credit derivative markets, dealer banks occupy a pivotal position as market makers and are also sellers of protection. Given the strong concentration which took place in the industry over the past 20 years, dealer banks with a large market share in the credit derivative market are likely to be, at the same time, systemic banks. As such they will be exposed to economic recessions and global crises. Therefore, as credit protection sellers—in the form of CDSs or other instruments—these dealer banks will most likely be the source of General Wrong-way risk.[8]

In a situation of deep economic recession or crisis, the risk of default and/or default events of dealer banks that are sellers of CDSs sharply increases due to the creditworthiness weaking of the corporates and entities on which they have sold protection, while their own credit quality is likely weakened by the global economic and/or financial downturn (either because of their exposure to weakened clients across all products, or because of their own market exposure as it happened in the 2007–2008 crisis). The clients of these dealer banks experience Wrong-way risk: They see the increase in the MtM of their credit derivatives—which is their exposure to the dealer bank—while the counterparty risk of the dealer bank increases at the same time

Put Option Put options sold by banks on a stock whose performance is correlated to their own credit quality (for instance another bank) offer another example, relatively similar to the CDS. During 2007–2008, most large dealers simultaneously experienced a dramatic fall in their stock prices. Those banks which were net sellers of CDS on banks were generating a very significant and worrisome Wrong-way risk for their clients. An extreme case of this would be a bank selling put options on their own name.

FX hedging swap for an emerging market investor Emerging government bond markets have materially expanded since 2000, in sync with the impressive performance of the most successful emerging economies (now referred to as the "BRICs" even if these successful emerging economies go beyond the initial list of the four "BRICs": Brazil, Russia, India, and China). Conservative investors such as Multilateral Development Banks (MDBs) would typically buy these bonds in local currency for their liquid portfolios and would swap them back into dollars or euros or other currencies. Their swap counterparties may be local banks, or else local subsidiaries of large global banks which are not explicitly guaranteed by their mother company. The MDB would be exposed to Wrong-way risk in the hedging currency swap (payer floating leg dollar and receiver fixed rate emerging currency). If the performance of the country significantly deteriorates, so does, at the same time, in all likelihood, the credit quality of the local bank taken as swap counterparty; at the same time, the local currency is likely to depreciate versus the dollar—therefore the value of the hedging swap, in which the local bank pays the local currency, increases from the MDB's side, and so does, at the same time, the exposure to the local bank.

Box 2: Wrong-way Risk in the AIG Case

The global insurance and financial company AIG with $1 trillion in assets, still rated AAA by the three rating agencies in 2005, lost $99 billion in 2008 and had to be rescued from bankruptcy, on September 16, 2008, by the Treasury, the Federal Reserve and the Federal Reserve of New York. Two lines of business precipitated the downfall: a) proprietary investments in RMBSs (Residential Mortgage Backed Securities) and real-estate CDOs

(Collateralized Debt Obligations); b) selling of credit protection via CDSs (Credit Default Swaps), for a total notional value of $527 billion in 2008. Out of the total $99 billion loss, these two business lines represented $50 billion in 2008; CDS on mortgage-related bonds alone amounted to $29 billion. With hindsight it appears that all counterparties holding CDSs offering protection on real estate that had been bought from AIG were exposed to Wrong-way risk. AIG was sitting on an excessively large and concentrated exposure to real estate. As AIG's real estate losses were adding up, so was the MtM of the CDSs AIG had written.

Real Estate Exposure year-end 2007 In $ Billion

	AIG	Citigroup	B of A
Total real estate exposure	380	475	569
As % of Adjusted Assets (%)	24	21	32
As % of Equity (%)	397	418	388

Source AIG in Hindsight. R. McDonald and A. Paulson, Federal Reserve Bank of Chicago, Oct. 2014

In most OTC derivatives, Wrong-way risk may simply stem from the counterparty's excess concentration on one type of risk. As explained above, a MtM loss to the counterparty in an OTC derivative contract—be it a currency swap, a sold stock put option, a commodity forward, or a CDS—should not in itself, because this loss marginally hampers the financial strength of the counterparty, generate Wrong-way risk. The reason is that, in principle, the counterparty has diversified the risks to which they are exposed. However, this is no longer true if the counterparty has accumulated a substantially concentrated position on exactly the same risk as the one embedded in the OTC derivative. The typical example is the case of credit insurance or "credit wraps" massively sold by AIG and insurance companies—*Monoline insurers*—during the 2007–2008 crisis (see Box 2).

4.2 Wrong-Way Risk Measure

The impact of Wrong-way risk should be reflected in both the measure of the expected loss on a derivative (which is the CVA, the Credit Value Adjustment, to be detailed in Chap. "Adjusting for Credit and Debt

Value: CVA and DVA") and the measure of the worst-case loss (which is the Economic or Regulatory Capital assigned to an OTC derivative). In both cases, the procedure will consist of establishing an explicit link—either algebraic or statistical—between two indicators: the one measuring the exposure and the one measuring the probability of default.

Let us be more specific. We will see in Chap. "Adjusting for Credit and Debt Value: CVA and DVA" that for a portfolio of derivatives between two entities A and B, the basic formula for the CVA, seen from the point of view of A is

$$CVA_A^B(t) = -LGD_B \sum_{t_i=t}^{T-1} PD_B(t_i, t_{i+1})\, EE_A^B(t_i) \tag{3}$$

With:

LGD_B	Loss Given Default on entity B;
$PD_B(t_i, t_{i+1})$:	Probability of Default of B in the future, in the time interval: $[t_i, t_{i+1}]$;
$EE_A^B(t_i)$:	Expected Exposure of A to B at the future time t_i, computed for all derivatives in the Netting Set and present-valued at time t;
T:	Maturity of the portfolio, i.e., maturity of the instrument with the longest tenor in the Netting Set

The modeling of Wrong-way risk will consist in establishing a connection in the computation of the future estimates of $EE_A^B(t_i)$ and $PD_B(t_i, t_{i+1})$.

For example, in a portfolio of CDSs buying protection on one entity or on a set of highly correlated entities.

If the future values of $EE_A^B(t_i)$ are obtained from estimating:

- The future probabilities of default of the underlying entity (ies) in the CDS (the one (s) the default of which protection has been purchased against), with these probabilities of default obtained from the future simulated values of a number of risk factors;
- The future paths of interest rates providing discount factors to compute the present value of the exposure.

Then, the future values of $PD_B(t_i, t_{i+1})$, the probabilities of default of the entity B selling the CDSs, should be estimated from the future values of risk factors, among which will feature factors that are the same as those determining the probabilities of default of the underlying counterparties.

In addition, one could also consider that the values of the interest rate should be factored in as determinants of probabilities of default (in a situation of economic crisis, as default rates increase across all economic sectors, interest rates would generally go down).

Notes

1. In the economic context of 2016, with negative interest rates in Europe questions were raised about the direction of payments in rate instruments. It is worth noting that market practice, in swap markets, states that a negative LIBOR or EURIBOR rate can reverse the direction of a payment, with the party paying EURIBOR actually receiving money, whereas interest on a floating rate note with a negative variable index would always remain positive.
2. BCBS: The Application of Basel II to Trading Activities and the Treatment of Double Default Effects, July 2005 (BCBS 2005).
3. Basel Committee on Banking Supervision, *Basel Capital Accord: Treatment of Potential Exposure for Off- Balance Sheet Items* (Basel, April 1995).
4. BCBS, Basel III: A global regulatory framework for more resilient banks and banking systems, June 2011.
5. J. Hull and A. White, *"Libor vs. OIS: The Derivatives Discounting Dilemma"*, 2013, Journal of Investment Management (Hull and White 2012).
6. J.P. Morgan, "*Wrong-way exposure*," Risk, June 1999); Finger, C., "*Toward a better estimation of wrong-way credit exposure*," Journal of Risk Finance, 2000.
7. September 7, 2001 from K. D'Hulster, Policy Director, ISDA to R. Gresser, Chairman of Counterparty Risk sub-group of the Models Task Force.
8. M. Pykhtin and A. Sokol: "*Exposure under Systemic Impact*," Risk, 2013.

References

BCBS. (2005, July). *The application of Basel II to trading activities and the treatment of double default effect.*

Hull, J., & White, A. (2012). LIBOR vs. OIS: The derivatives discounting dilemma. *Journal of Investment Management* 2015, draft April 2013.

Pykhtin, M., & Sokol, A. (2013). Exposure under systemic impact. *Risk, 26.*

Restating the Role of Collateral

Abstract This chapter documents the practice of collateral posting in derivative markets, introduced at the onset to provide protection against the potential default of a counterparty, and which has evolved into an art: selecting instruments—cash or securities—eligible as collateral, settling disputes, and minimizing costs. The liquidity risk stemming from the obligation to post collateral, or Margin Call Risk, has contributed to the collapse of several large firms (the case of Metallgesellschaft is reviewed). Post-2008 regulation significantly tightens collateral posting rules in order to remove all shortcomings existing in the protection against default risk. The Chapter documents how regulation leaves flexibility in the practice of collateral re-use (or re-hypothecation) so as to help collateral "circulate" and remain available, and to help participants minimize its cost.

Keywords Collateral amount (Received or Posted) · Margin call (Risk)
Variation margin · Initial margin · ISDA master agreement · CCP central clearing counterparty · CSA credit support annex · Eligible instrument
Threshold · IA independent amount · Swap end-user swap dealer
Margin period of risk · Haircut · Re-hypothecation · Segregation

I. Zelenko, *Credit Risk Management for Derivatives*,
DOI 10.1007/978-3-319-57975-7_3

1 The Destination of Collateral

1.1 The Concept: A Dynamic and Symmetric Protection Against Counterparty Risk

Derivatives were introduced in the late 1970s and early 1980s to answer the need to manage market price risk, as interest rate and currency volatility was becoming the norm. Derivatives soon became indispensable—an integral part of capital markets. At the same time, derivatives were simply contracts among two parties, contracts whose value, constantly changing over time, had to be protected against the possibility of default.

Posting collateral was found to be the most effective way to provide protection against the risk of default of the parties to a derivative contract. Collateral has also the property to mitigate default in the dynamic context of derivative in which the value of the contract and the exposure changes over time.

The posting of collateral by one counterparty to a derivative contract means transferring to the other counterparty an amount in cash—or quasi-cash in the form of safe and liquid securities—equal to the value (or MtM or Mark-to-Market) of the contract when this value becomes negative and represents a claim and an exposure to the other counterparty.

A derivative contract continuously changes in value (MtM) over its life (see Chap. "Outlining Counterparty Credit Risk Exposure"): The MtM will experience significant fluctuations in value and may change sign. So the posting of collateral has to be dynamic too. The two parties to an OTC derivative contract, if the trade is uncleared (i.e., not cleared on a central clearing counterparty or CCP), will have to post collateral to each other during the life of the trade to mitigate default risk.

The two parties to an over-the-counter (OTC) derivative contract would normally include an end-user (institutional investor, corporate, financial agency, or a commercial bank), and a derivative dealer. We will see, later in this chapter, that derivative dealers, being in practice parties to every transaction, have performed a special role in centralizing collateral flows.

A derivative contract would generally start with an initial MtM[1] covered by a payment in cash, if an option, or with no initial value (zero MtM), if a future or a swap.

For example, in buying a 1-year OTC call option on the Dow Jones Index from counterparty B, counterparty A would pay to B, on start date, the MtM of the option, while receiving from B, on the same day, the call option, whose initial MtM is equal to the effected payment. In the case of this option, there is exposure from day one, since the option starts with a positive MtM. So B has to post collateral to A from the onset. If the collateral is paid in cash, B would transfer back to A the cash received against the option.

As for swaps, they would normally start with a zero value. In a fixed versus floating dollar interest rate swap, the rate on the fixed leg would normally be set so that the value of the swap on start date is zero. There would be no need payment at inception, and there would also be neither exposure nor collateral payment.

But immediately after the start date, the swap MtM will continuously change. And for the two parties, depending on the sign of the MtM, the swap contract may represent alternatively an exposure or a debt. This symmetric feature is one of the key aspects of counterparty credit risk exposure. Every time A has a positive MtM, A has counterparty credit risk exposure to B—A would suffer a capital loss, equal to the MtM, if B were to default. To offset this exposure, the swap contract requires B to post a collateral amount to A, in cash or in safe securities, equal to the MtM.[2] When the MtM increases, A asks for additional collateral, and B has to answer this collateral call or variation margin or "margin call" (see Fig. 1). If B were to not answer the margin call, B would be in default. But A would already have received collateral for a large fraction of the MtM.

1.2 The Adoption: Collateral as a Standard of OTC Derivatives

Collateral has been introduced early on in OTC derivatives markets. While margining was a defining feature of future and option exchanges, posting collateral started as a practice in OTC derivative trading, then evolved to become a standard set of contractual clauses commonly agreed by swap dealers and swap market participants, a.k.a. "The industry." Their representative body, the International Swap and Derivatives

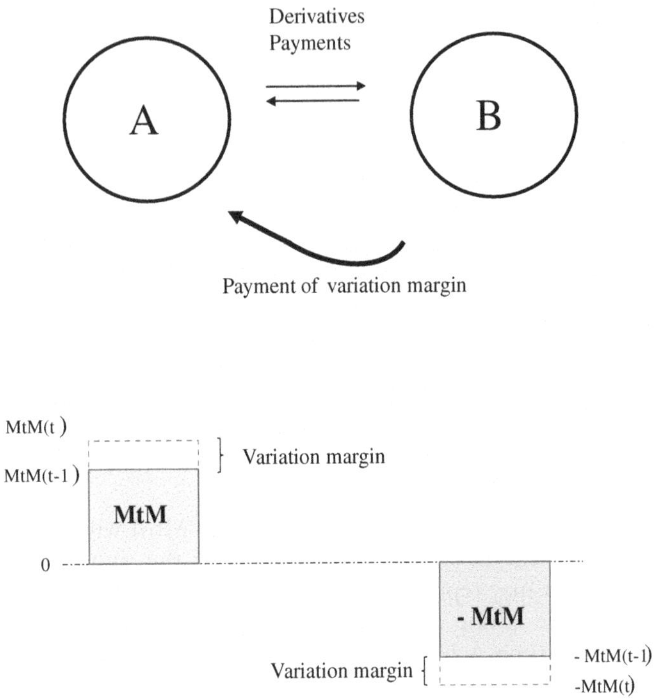

Fig. 1 Additional flow of payments due to collateral calls (or variation margins)

Association or ISDA,[3] founded in 1985, has been the forum where standards have been discussed and adopted over the past thirty years.

In its own words, the ISDA "has worked to make the global derivatives markets safer and more efficient" and "has helped to significantly reduce credit and legal risk." Together with increasing transparency and improving infrastructure, reducing counterparty credit risk has been a key priority. The first ISDA Master Agreement published in 1994 established legal standards for all derivative OTC contracts, and in particular established standards for the Credit Support Annex (CSA), the section in the contract which gathers all clauses pertaining to credit risk and collateral.[4] As of today, the 1994 ISDA Master Agreement constitutes the reference set of practices and rules. These have evolved over time under the auspices of the ISDA and, sometimes, as a result of the regulatory action, as is the case at present, in the aftermath of the 2007–2008 crisis.

The use of collateral by swap and derivative market participants has been widespread and continuously increasing until 2013. Graph 1 below shows the ISDA survey-based statistics of estimated amounts of collateral in OTC derivatives markets from 1999 to 2013. Their trend follows the growth of derivatives transactions. After 2008, however, the impact of the crisis and the introduction of the central clearing counterparty (CCP) have taken transactions and collateral away from the OTC market. According to the ISDA, there was, at the end of 2013 147,562 bilateral collateral agreements (versus 70,892 in 2005), an estimated $3.2 trillion collateral in circulation for OTC non-cleared transactions, 90% of which were collateralized versus 59% in 2006, and 30% only in 2003. The actual decrease in the total outstanding amount of OTC derivatives in 2015 (see Chaps. "Reshaping Derivatives Markets: The Post-2008 Ambition" and "Outlining Counterparty Credit Risk Exposure") must have been matched by the corresponding reduction in collateral amount.

Swap dealers, banks, security firms, institutional investors (asset managers, mutual funds, insurance companies and pension funds, hedge funds), and governments and government agencies would generally rely on collateral agreements in their OTC derivative trading activity (the proportion of entities with a CSA in each of these categories is in the 81–93% range). However, only about a third of non-financial institutions, which include corporates, would have a CSA.

Collateral posting is prevalent in securitized borrowing markets. In a repo, the borrower would borrow cash from a market counterparty while posting a security of a high credit quality, generally a government bond: This allows the borrower to benefit from the borrowing spread of the least risky signature.

Collateral posting or margining is mandatory when trading derivatives on a future or option exchange or clearing on a CCP. Participants have to post an initial margin and then pay variation margins as their MtM becomes more negative. One does not receive collateral from an exchange or a CCP, which instead collects collateral from the counterparty to trade and can therefore guarantee against default.

1.3 The Implementation: Key Clauses in the CSA

In this section, we examine the rules governing collateral, gathered in the CSA. We will ask these rules two questions:

(i) Do they effectively protect against default?
(ii) Do they minimize the cost of this protection?

The CSA states:

(i) ***The scope:*** the MtM and resulting exposure are computed on a *Netting Set* of transactions;
(ii) ***The exposure:*** derived from the net value or MtM of all outstanding swaps and derivatives included in the Netting Set, with a MtM calculation based on the mid-market value, taken from public sources such as brokers' screens, of all market variables determining the MtM;
(iii) ***The periodicity of variation margin payments:*** daily posting is the norm since 2008.
(iv) ***The eligible instruments*** deemed acceptable (generally cash and government securities).

Collateral is not strictly equal to the MtM. Exposure can be reduced below the MtM by applying a *Threshold*; it can be expanded beyond the MtM by imposing the payment of an *Independent Amount* (IA). Both the Threshold and the IA depend on the creditworthiness of the counterparty, as measured by its rating.

The *Threshold* and the *Independent Amount* are rating-dependent in the CSA and would also be made entity-dependent by a market participant, which may have a perception of counterparty risk which goes beyond the rating of rating agencies and considers the nature of the entity. For instance, a swap end-user may consider an AAA-rated *Derivative Subsidiary* of a dealer bank or an AAA-rated *Special Purpose Entity* as riskier than an AAA financial firm or an AAA corporate (see Table 1).

The *Threshold* sets the minimum MtM from where collateral should be posted. It is destined to reduce the operational burden of collateral posting by avoiding cash and security transfers as long as the exposure remains low. An entity with an AAA rating would obtain the highest threshold (except for certain entities—see para above). A strong AAA such as a government or an International Financial Organization would

Table 1 Threshold and Independent Amount rules for a Swap End-User

Rating	*Threshold*			
	Independent Amount (IA)			
	Commercial Bank	*Broker Dealer*	*Derivative Subsidiary*	*Insurance Company*
AAA	300	100	100	100
AA+	250	80	0	80
AA	200	60	0	60
AA-	100	40	0	40
A+	50	20	0	20
A	25	10	IA	10
A-	10	0	IA	IA
BBB + & below	IA	IA	IA	IA

In million US dollar

normally benefit from an infinite Threshold (i.e., no collateral posting). In the same vein, the Minimum Transfer Amount specifies the minimum amount by which the MtM should change to trigger a variation margin; it would be usually set in the 1 million US dollar range or less. A typical Threshold scale would be as per below (see Table 1):

The *Independent Amount* (IA) payment is triggered in case of a downgrade, generally from BBB + or BBB, and according to the CSA clauses. It is an essential protection against the default of a counterparty. This over-collateralization mechanism has been customary since the early days of the swap market in the 1980s. Originally, the IA was applicable only to end-users in derivatives markets, particularly hedge funds or those with low credit ratings, in order to protect dealer banks, which have long benefited from a strong credit quality, and from good ratings. In its *March 2010 White Paper on Independent Amount*, the ISDA outlines the very purpose of IA, designed to guard against the following residual credit risk of collateralized derivative transaction, which may occur in four typical situations (see Box 1).

Box 1: Residual risks covered by the IA

1. When mark-to-market fluctuations occur, there is a delay before the new collateral amount can be computed, called and settled.
2. When a counterparty defaults, no more collateral movements will occur but credit exposure may continue to increase until the non-defaulting party closes out the relevant risk positions.
3. Collateral agreements typically contain structural features designed to ensure that effort and cost are not wasted in moving *de minimis* amounts of collateral between the parties.
4. Collateral transfers under the CSA are based on mid-market values of the underlying derivative contracts, whereas a party's loss upon default of the other party may be realized at either the bid or offer side of the market. Thus, some disparity between collateral and exposure is always to be expected, and this may be significant where spreads for a product are particularly wide.

Source ISDA White Paper on Independent Amount March 2010.

The most direct use of the IA as a counterparty risk mitigant is to protect against a potential increase in MtM, going much beyond the collateral held, during the *Margin Period of Risk*. This risk is measured by a 10-day or a 20-day Potential Future Exposure (PFE).

Swap end-users would therefore define the IA to be posted when triggered based on a PFE calculation. Since PFE estimates are calculated using proprietary models, which may differ or may not be accessible, the CSA could feature a simplified approximated formula on which the two parties can agree.

In fact, the US regulation on margining published in September 2016 (see Chap. "Reshaping Derivatives Markets: The Post-2008 Ambition") has required that an *Initial Margin*, equal to the PFE computed over the Margin Period of Risk, be exchanged among dealers. This means that an IA has now become mandatory among two swap dealers and the Initial Margin amounts cannot be netted. This requirement, applicable to all in the interdealer market, has triggered the development of a specific infrastructure for swap dealers to agree on the Initial Margin amount to be paid. The SIMM, *Standard Initial Margin Model for Uncleared Derivatives*, an open-source model which computes a PFE over the Margin Period of Risk, has been sponsored by major US swap dealers.

The SIMM uses a simplified formula to estimate the Initial Margin and allows swap dealers to reach agreement. In terms of risk management, it is also a welcome effort by the industry to foster the simplification and standardization of CCR risk metrics.

2 The Art of Managing Collateral

Collateral management has become more demanding during the 2000 decade, as the creditworthiness of swap dealers was unceasingly deteriorating while posting collateral was growing as a concern. For many banks, collateral management has moved from a back-office operational process to take part in key Treasury front office functions.

There are two sides to collateral management, which are closely linked: obtain effective protection when *receiving collateral*; minimize the cost of *posting collateral.*

2.1 The Art of Receiving Collateral: The Credit Support Amount (CSA)

Except when one of the counterparties is smaller than the other, the amount to be received on a collateral call date, or "Credit Support Amount," is determined by the collateral receiver acting as valuation agent. The calculation will involve the following steps: (i) calculating the MtM of the swap and/or derivative portfolio on the netting set covered by the ISDA contract; (ii) calculating the change in the MtM of the securities received as collateral (net of haircuts applicable); (iii) determining the new uncollateralized exposure and, based on threshold and minimum transfer amount clauses, computing the collateral call. A netting set could include not only fixed income, equity, foreign exchange, commodity, and credit derivatives (using the ISDA classification) but also structured derivatives, hybrid, weather, or catastrophe instruments.

2.2 The Art of Receiving Collateral: Settling Disputes

A disagreement on the valuation, more likely to happen on the most complex and least liquid instruments, can trigger a dispute (See Figs 2 and 3). A large-sized swap market participant would typically face a dispute on a weekly basis. Usually, these are "good faith" disputes which are resolved within one or two business days. But a counterparty could

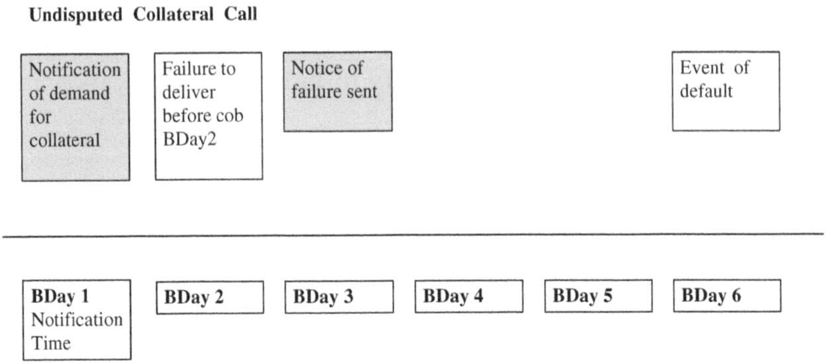

Fig. 2 Sequence of events in an unmet collateral call

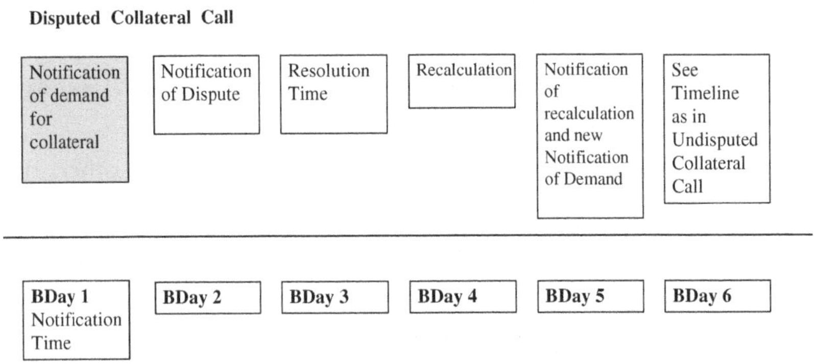

Fig. 3 Sequence of events in a dispute on a collateral call

also attempt to delay delivery of any collateral for an indefinite period of time (a "bad-faith" dispute). In such a case, the front office or, if needed, the senior management would first be alerted and would try to resolve the dispute in an "unofficial" way. Otherwise the CSA *Dispute Resolution* paragraph could be used, something both parties would normally seek to avoid, however.

If a demand for collateral is made (on Notification Time), and if the counterparty fails to deliver the collateral before close of business on the next business day, the collateral receiver may invoke an Event of Default and would then need to first give notice of the failed delivery to the

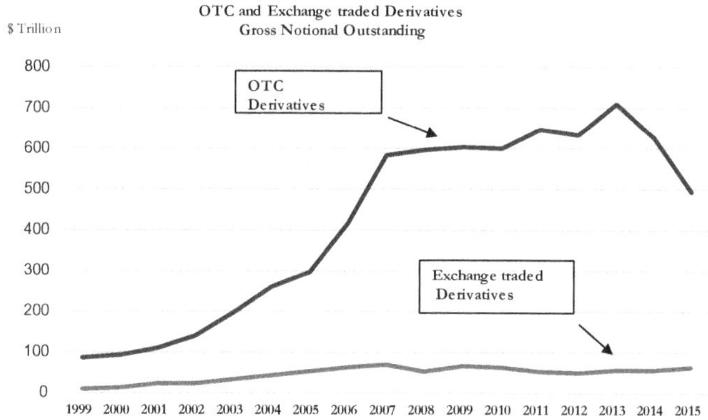

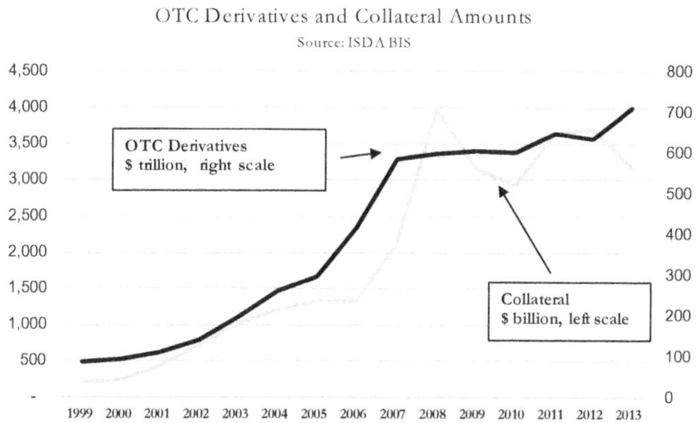

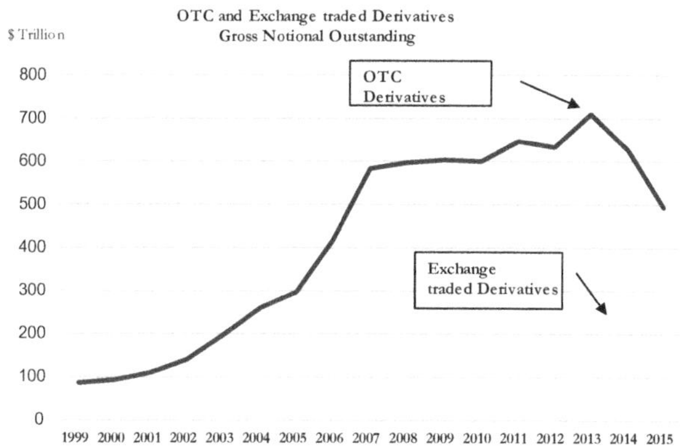

Graph 1 Evolution of Total Outstanding Amounts in OTC Derivatives and Collateral. *Source*: BIS derivatives statistics; ISDA Margin Surveys 2014 and 2006

collateral payer. Default happens if the counterparty continues its failure during two business days after receiving notice. The default notably gives the right to the collateral receiver to terminate the ISDA agreement. This is an "undisputed collateral call."

The collateral payer may choose, however, to formally dispute the amount required: This would be a "disputed collateral call." In this case, the dispute must be notified before the close of the business day following the Notification Time.

The parties must resolve the dispute by Resolution Time—1:00 pm on the business day following the date on which the dispute has been notified. If the dispute has not been resolved by such Resolution Time, the collateral receiver must obtain four quotations for the MtM, from four dealer banks, recalculate the MtM as the arithmetic average, then resend a collateral call based on this new MtM. The collateral payer would then have to deliver collateral based on the timeline described in the Undisputed Collateral Call case.

2.3 The Art of Receiving Collateral: Eligible Instruments

The CSA specifies the list of instruments considered as eligible collateral (see Table 2). The 2014 ISDA Margin Survey gives the following information on collateral in cleared and uncleared derivative transactions. Cash in dollar and euro is still the predominant form of collateral for OTC derivatives. Government bonds are accepted to the extent they are "as good as cash." From the counterparty credit protection standpoint, only securities that can be rapidly and safely converted into cash—i.e., highly safe and liquid—are accepTable. During the 2007-08 crisis, the sharp deterioration in credit quality, and in market acceptance, of AAA-rated signatures mostly perceived to be as safe as governments have narrowed the scope of eligible instruments. In Table 2 below, which gives the percentages of various types of collateral, US Government Sponsored Entities (or GSEs: Fannie Mae, Freddie Mac etc.) represent 16% of the 10.3% of "Other Securities" received as collateral. By comparison, in the same ISDA Survey of 2006, 21% of respondents declared they were accepting agency paper as collateral.

When securities are received as collateral, an essential aspect is to be protected against a reduction in their market price at the time a default happens. This protection takes the form of an extra amount requested by the collateral receiver, above and beyond the MtM: the *haircut*.

Table 2 Composition of collateral received against non-cleared and cleared transactions. *Source* ISDA Margin Survey 2014

		OTC Derivatives	
As of December 31, 2013		*Uncleared*	*Cleared**
Cash		**74.9%**	**66.6%**
	Dollar	31.7%	60.5%
	Euro	36.5%	4.5%
	Yen	2.4%	0.0%
	Pound	1.9%	1.1%
	Other	2.5%	0.3%
Government Bonds		**14.8%**	**30.8%**
	United States	4.3%	23.3%
	European Union	3.0%	0.0%
	Japan	2.9%	0.0%
	United Kingdom	1.6%	1.1%
	Other	3.0%	6.4%
Other Securities		**10.3%**	**2.6%**

*Received to meet Initial Margin

The *haircut* is a discount applied to the market price of a security received as collateral to account for:

1. a potential rapid decrease in market price;
2. a liquidity quality situated below that of the most liquid government bonds.

Regarding market risk (point 1. Above), the longer the maturity (the duration), the higher the haircut, which can be 10% for bonds with maturities above 10 years.

Other aspects that determine the haircut would be the correlation between the credit quality of the counterparty, in the absolute and also relative to the security received (including government bonds).

Example 1:

Application of a 5% haircut to a bond

Bond's face value:	$40 M
Market price:	102
Bond's MtM (a):	$40.8 M
Haircut (b):	$2.04 M
Collateral value (a—b):	$38.76 M

The credit quality and the liquidity of the collateral received also considerably matter from the standpoint of minimizing the cost of posting collateral.

2.4 The Art of Posting Collateral: Minimizing the Cost

Taken in isolation, the action of posting collateral implies a cost because the collateral posted (if it is cashed) or delivered (if it is securities) has to be borrowed or sourced (see Figs 4 and 5).

The dealer bank in Fig. 4 posts cash (75% of collateral received in OTC derivatives) in dollar. According to market practice, the dealer is paid the Fed Funds rate, which is the average rate at which banks lend to each other overnight on an unsecured basis. A swap dealer bank, with a weaker credit quality than the average, would pay a spread over the average Fed Fund rate. The same reasoning would apply for euro cash, with the EONIA rate playing the role of the Fed Fund.

The asset manager may decide, on the other hand, to deliver a US Treasury taken from its portfolio. But the asset manager loses the return it would obtain by using the same UST bond to borrow in a repo transaction and invest in a short-term (non-government) security. The asset manager also weakens its liquidity position since the UST bond note is no longer available to obtain funding via a repo.

The asset manager or any financial institution posting a security as collateral would normally choose, among all securities accepted as collateral, the *cheapest to deliver*. The "cheapest" would be determined according to

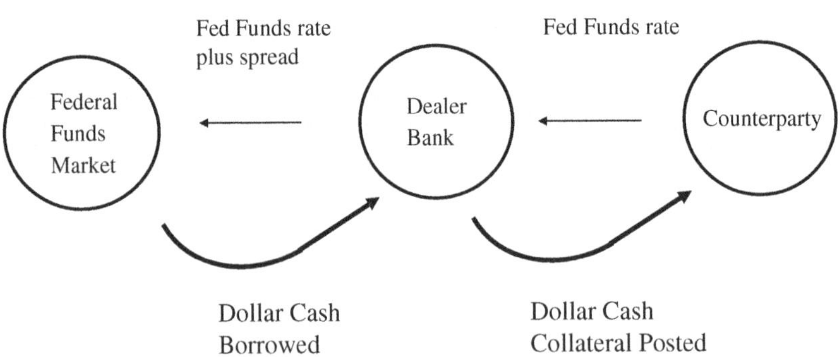

Fig. 4 Dealer bank borrowing and posting dollar cash collateral

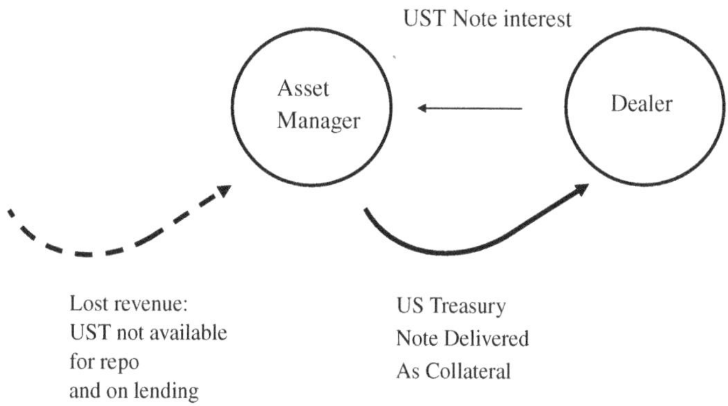

Fig. 5 Asset Manager posting a US Treasury note as collateral

several criteria such as the liquidity or the acceptability as collateral of the security. The security posted can also be a security received as collateral and re-hypothecated (see below).

The haircut applied by the counterparties posting and receiving collateral plays an important role in this optimization. Note that a dealer bank, which would operate exclusively as a broker (all derivatives positions are fully hedged), would be expected to receive as much collateral as they would have to post if all CSAs are identical, in particular regarding the threshold and haircut clauses. But these clauses may differ among counterparties and create asymmetries.[5] In any event, every swap and derivative market participant should centralize the management of the net position in collateral owed or received. Since 2008, dealer banks and financial institutions have given heightened consideration to the management of collateral at the balance sheet's level as this may have major implications for the overall funding of the firm and its liquidity position.

2.5 *The Art of Posting Collateral: Re-Hypothecation*

With the intention of minimizing collateral costs via the optimal management of collateral flows, the possibility to reuse as *pledger* (collateral payer) securities received as *pledgee* (collateral receiver) is of paramount importance. But the right to such reuse or re-hypothecation must have been given in the ISDA contract (in the CSA).

The majority of ISDA contracts are established under New York Law (47.6%) or English Law (28.3%).[6] This results in two separate legal regimes.

Under English Law, the transfer of collateral is a *title transfer*. There is a transfer of ownership, so, within certain restrictions, the pledgee can use the security received as they see fit. The security can be re-hypothecated as collateral or even sold. However, the pledgee has the obligation to return the same or an *equivalent* security: this possibility of a replacement, called *substitution*, should be agreed by both parties.[7]

Under New York Law, the transfer of collateral is a *pledge*. The pledger remains the owner of the security or cash. The pledgee acquires certain rights, such as receiving ownership upon default by the pledger. The right to re-hypothecate must be explicitly given by the pledger in the CSA.

Collateral re-hypothecation is a standard practice. But this may be reserved to market participants having the required operational capacity. For instance, it is essential for a firm that customarily reuses securities pledged as collateral to be able to differentiate, among all securities received, those for which the pledger has granted re-hypothecation rights from those delivered without this right.

Re-hypothecation makes collateral similar to money. The same amount of collateral can support a multiple amount of transactions, so one can think of the reuse of collateral in the same way as of the velocity of money. This aspect has notably been analyzed by the IMF economist Manmohan Singh, which estimated the total amount of collateral received to $10 trillion in 2007 and $5.8 trillion in 2010.[8] Singh has

Table 3 Report on Collateral Re-hypothecation Activity—Goldman Sachs June 2015

The Table below presents financial instruments at fair value received as collateral that were available to be delivered or re-pledged and were delivered or re-pledged by the firm. As of June 2015 in $ thousands

Collateral available to be delivered or re-pledged:	$33,653,567
Collateral that was delivered or re-pledged:	$28,993,717

As of June 2015, amounts exclude $496.2 million of securities received under resale agreements that contractually had the right to be delivered or re-pledged, but were segregated to satisfy certain regulatory requirements

Source: GOLDMAN SACHS EXECUTION & CLEARING, L.P. Notes to Statement of Financial Condition (Unaudited)

focused on the availability or scarcity of collateral needed to support OTC derivatives and repo transactions. The extract of the financial reporting of Goldman Sachs below (see Table 3) shows how a dealer bank would report on its activities in collateral management and also shows the size (around $30 billion in the case of Goldman Sachs).

3 The Shortcomings of Collateral and the Margin Call Risk

Collateral cannot fully eradicate counterparty risk. Per current market practice, collateralization mechanisms in OTC markets do not achieve complete protection against the default of a counterparty. Collateral was born with a number of flaws. We will review those in the first paragraph of this section. In addition, and even assuming these flaws have been addressed, risk cannot just go away. Collateral first converts risk into costs: operational costs, legal costs, and funding costs. Even more concerning, risk itself has not disappeared. Rather it has morphed into another major risk: liquidity risk.

3.1 Collateralization Shortcomings

3.1.1 Replacement Risk and PFE

The first limitation in the protection brought by collateral has to do with what happens immediately after default. Outside of the case of a resolution, all derivatives and swaps, upon default of one of the parties, and under the terms of the ISDA contract, have to be terminated. All swaps in the netting set should be canceled against the due payment of the MtM of the portfolio. But all of these terminated derivatives were performing a specific role in the balance sheet of the entity confronted with the default of its counterparty. This overall derivatives' position has to be *replaced* as rapidly as possible by another position having characteristics matching or most closely replicating those of the derivatives portfolio terminated upon default. All sensitivities of the MtM—deltas, gammas, and others—must be restored at the earliest. Just as crucially, the MtM itself has to be reinstated in the replacing position, at the identical, avoiding any loss.

The default generates indeed, at the time of default, an open position for the surviving entity. Replacing the defaulted position is not instantaneous. A dealer bank would enter into transactions in a limited number of instruments and markets to hedge the position globally, on a portfolio basis. On the other hand, several financial institutions may have to replace single-handedly every instrument in a portfolio of several hundreds of swap or derivative contracts.

This critical time during which the entity is exposed to uncontrolled market risk because of an open position, while the defaulted derivatives are being hedged or replaced is called the *Replacement Period* or *Margin Period of Risk*. Regulation recommends to estimate this period to be 10 business days for a portfolio of standard or vanilla swaps and derivatives, or 20 business days if there are structured and/or illiquid instruments in the portfolio.

An entity with a positive MtM, a positive exposure, even if fully collateralized at the time of default (assuming therefore a zero threshold), will be exposed to the risk of the MtM materially increasing over the collateral held at the moment of default before the position can be replaced.

If the MtM of the position is positive at the time of default, the surviving entity has to pay a dealer bank the MtM to replace the defaulting counterparty. The surviving entity holds collateral equal to this MtM. But it is exposed to the *Replacement Risk* described above. Eventually, the *Replacement Cost* will include what the surviving entity has to pay over and above the collateral held to replace the position.

The *Replacement Risk* is measured by a PFE computed over the *Margin Period of Risk*, so either a 10-day or a 20-day PFE. Financial institutions would generally compute the PFE at the 95% or 99% level.

This *Replacement Risk* is the part of the counterparty credit risk not covered by the collateralization, except if an *Independent Amount* had been added to the CSA. The IAwould be triggered by the downgrade of the counterparty, below a predefined threshold. The IA normally allows a good protection against the Replacement Risk, but this assumes that the defaulting counterparty has been downgrading below the IA threshold prior to default. The IA tends to be defined by a formula representing an approximation of the PFE, but, again cannot be received if the defaulting counterparty has not been downgraded below the rating that triggers the IA. Ratings of Lehman just before it filed for bankruptcy (S&P: A; Moody's: A2; Fitch: A +) were not triggering any IA. The new margining regulation in the US, which went into force in September 2016, makes it mandatory, in the interdealer market, to post an IA as an Initial Margin.

In addition to the market risk measured by the 10- or 20-day PFE, the *Replacement Cost* may also reflect several other aspects. For instance, even if the MtM does not change, the payment to the new dealer bank may go well above the MtM measured at mid-market, because of a significant widening of the bid-ask spread whereas the collateral held by the surviving entity was computed based on the mid-market MtM. This will be all the more pronounced if the swap to be replaced is structured, bespoke or not commonly traded. Lehman was very involved in the market for structured notes or MTNs: Medium Term Notes, and in particular in JPY denominated notes having complex options on Japanese exchange rates (versus dollar, euro or other currencies) embedded. The dislocation of markets following Lehman's default was such that the payments needed to replace these swaps were largely in excess of any estimated 20-day PFE (see Fig. 6).

The same illustration in the case the IA clause had been triggered by the downgrading of the defaulting counterparty to BBB + prior to default shows the effectiveness of an IA defined as a simplified 10-day or 20-day PFE calculation (see Fig. 7).

A negative MtM can also give rise to an exposure and a loss because the MtM, during the Replacement Period, can increase to the point when it becomes positive, whereas no collateral has been received (see Fig. 8).

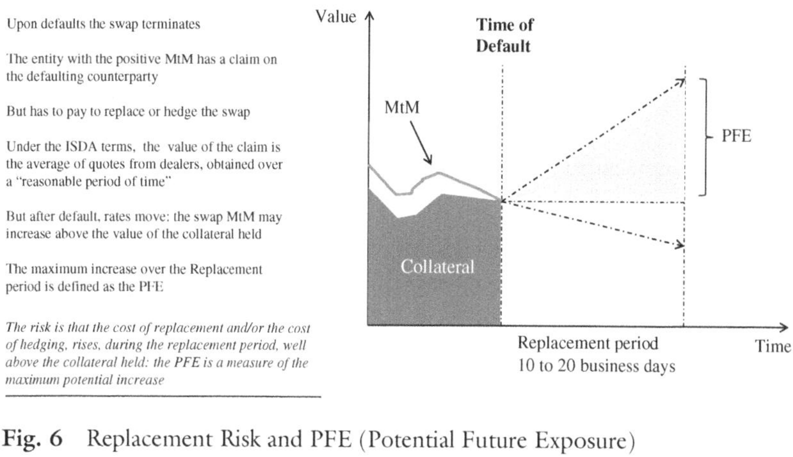

Fig. 6 Replacement Risk and PFE (Potential Future Exposure)

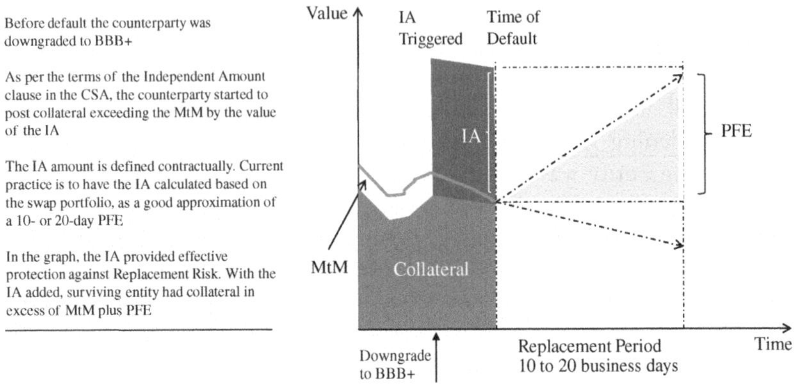

Fig. 7 Replacement Risk, PFE, and IA

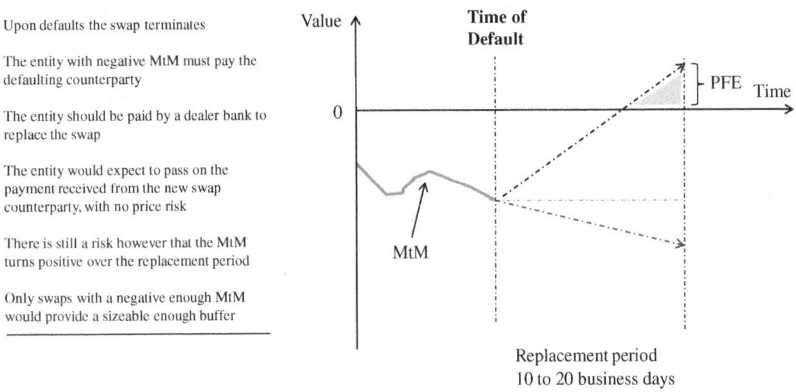

Fig. 8 Replacement Risk when the MtM is negative at the time of default

3.1.2 Credit Risk on Posted Collateral

Counterparty Credit Risk possesses an inherent property of symmetry. Over the life of a swap, an entity may go through periods when it has a positive MtM and has to watch its exposure and the collateral received. Yet, at a future stage, the same entity, in the same swap may have a negative MtM, having, in turn, to post collateral. This collateral, posted with the counterparty in the form of cash or in the form of government bonds, constitutes in itself an exposure in case of default (see Fig. 9).

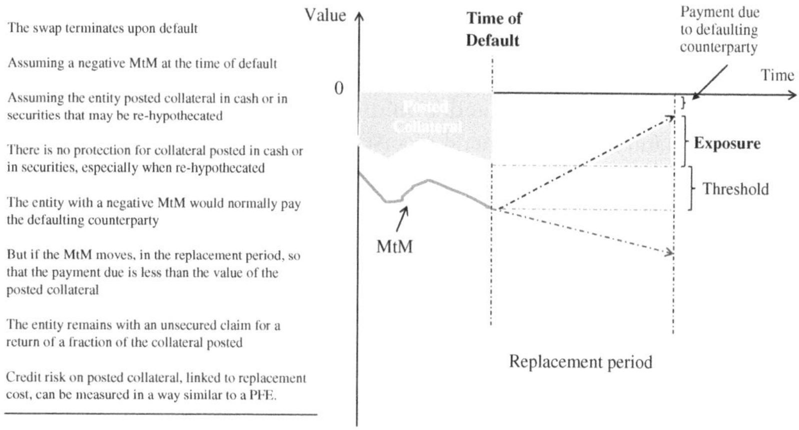

Fig. 9 Counterparty Exposure on posted collateral

If collateral posted to the defaulting counterparty is cash, the surviving entity will be *pari passu* with all other creditors having a claim on the net residual value of the bankrupt counterparty. The entity is in the situation of a loss upon default, striving for the recovery of its claim. It the collateral posted consists of securities, except in the case where a robust segregation scheme was created, the result is the same. This is particularly true if the securities have been re-hypothecated.

Of course, one has to remember that the collateral posted to the defaulting counterparty was of the same value of the negative MtM. The surviving entity is entitled to pay this negative MtM to the defaulting counterparty only if its collateral had been returned. Fine. But again, this reassuring equation may change a lot during the Replacement Period. This is because the MtM may have changed before the swap is replaced. Because it had a negative MtM the surviving entity would have to be paid by the new counterparty, replacing the defaulting one in the swap. But the payment may end up being less than the value of the collateral posted. The surviving entity ends up with a net claim on the defaulted counterparty, which would likely only be partially recovered (see Fig. 9).

Such counterparty risk on posted collateral, when collateral equals the negative MtM (minus threshold) can therefore be measured in the same way as a collateralized swap exposure, using a 10-day or 2-day PFE (Fig. 9).

But counterparty risk on collateral that is posted in excess of the MtM, such as the Independent Amount (IA) or any initial margin, is measured like an outright exposure. The collateral pledger in that case is exposed for the full amount and would end up with an unsecured claim in case of default by the collateral receiver.

3.1.3 Re-Hypothecation or Segregation

The wide spread practice of re-hypothecation aggravates counterparty risk on posted collateral. Securities posted as collateral to a dealer bank, and for which the right to re-pledge has been granted, are very likely to have been reused at the time of default and, in order to recover these securities, the pledging party would have no other choice than to track down their successive re-hypothecations. Figure 10 shows how the same US Treasury bond delivered by a financial institution to a swap dealer could "travel" through the financial system. When going through the bankruptcy process of Lehman in 2008, many clients of Lehman customarily posting collateral, among which many hedge funds, had been confronted with the highly difficult task to retrieve the assets they had posted (see Fig. 10).

Regulatory reforms undertaken after 2009 have attempted, among other things, to eliminate the practice of re-hypothecation by centralizing swap and derivatives trading on Central Clearing Counterparties (CCPs) which would receive and centralize all collateral and would not re-hypothecate it. Nevertheless, a large fraction of derivatives is still traded outside of CCPs. How can re-hypothecation be dealt with?

In OTC derivatives markets, an end-user willing to mitigate counterparty risk on posted collateral may decide to rely on segregation and, when negotiating the CSA with dealer banks, may require that

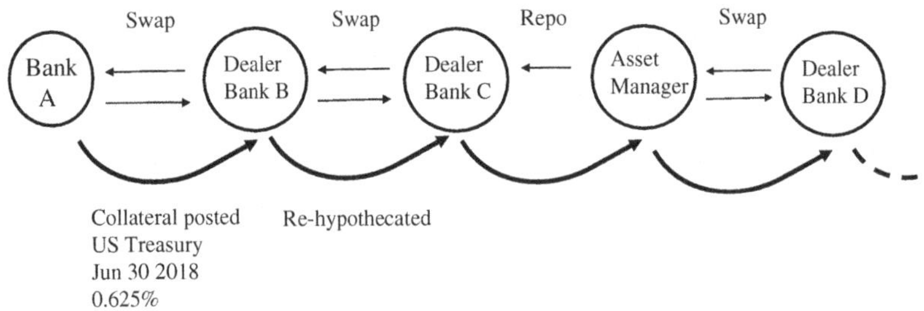

Fig. 10 Circulation of collateral

the collateral they would post be segregated, and be effectively made immune to the bankruptcy of the dealer bank. In fact, post-2008 regulations in the USA (Dodd-Frank) and in Europe (EMIR) require that swap dealers inform their counterparties of the right to segregate the initial margin with an independent third party.

Collateral segregation can take three forms:

- Segregation on the books of the secured party; in the case of a bankruptcy, however, collateral may still be lost;
- Segregation in a Third-Party custody agreement, in which an independent (unaffiliated) bank, appointed by one of the parties, holds the collateral received and provides custody and safekeeping services;
- Segregation in a tri-party collateral account: A third-party custodian bank (preferably with a strong rating) signs a three-way contract with both parties and acts as collateral keeper and manager.

The ISDA Independent Amount paper highlights the tri-party custodial agreement as an effective means for end-users to be protected against the loss of an initial margin or IA in the case of a default by their counterparty dealer bank.[9]

Segregation is an effective way to insulate posted collateral against counterparty risk. But it has a cost. A prudent financial institution that would systematically request swap dealers to segregate their posted collateral would generate a cost to these dealers. This would simply be the cost of funding collateral, currently measured by the FVA (see Chap. "Expanding Valuation Metrics:FVA and KVA"). The swap dealer which is the counterparty to the prudent financial institution would have to be hedged. When the MtM is positive with their client—the prudent financial institution—the MtM is negative in their hedge: They have to post collateral but they cannot use the segregated securities posted by the prudent financial institution or prudent FI in Fig. 11 (see Fig. 11).

The dealer will bear the funding cost. But then the prudent FI will be charged for this cost. So counterparty risk on collateral cannot be mitigated at no cost by segregation. This is because segregation breaks the "funding chain" of re-hypothecated collateral. The cost to the prudent FI would be similar to the cost the most creditworthy governments or AAA international financial institutions would pay in theory when they do not post collateral due to their high credit quality.

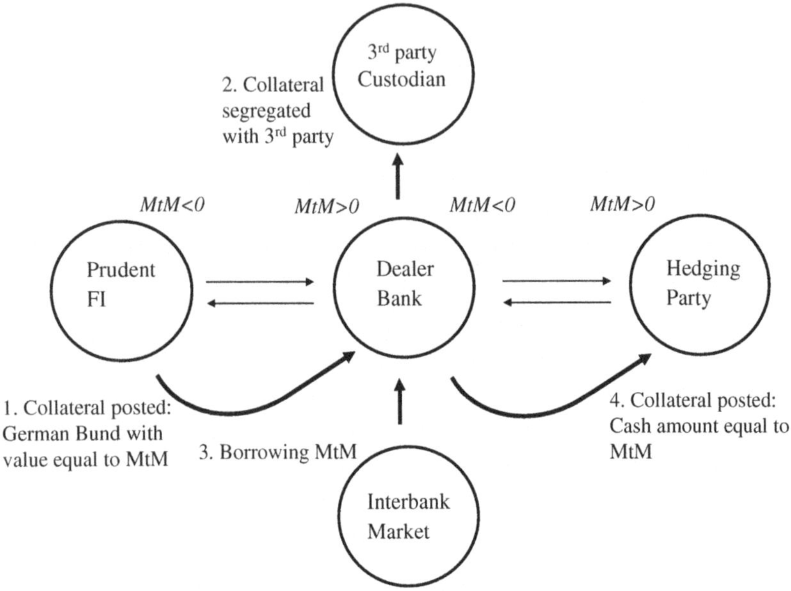

Fig. 11 Borrowing cost induced by segregation

So, there is a trade-off and a choice to make between re-hypothecation and segregation.

Segregation reduces counterparty risk but comes at a cost. It would be an industry-wide transaction cost if it were generalized and might be even more than that: It could lead to a shortage of collateral and a reduction in the liquidity of derivatives markets.[10]

Re-hypothecation accentuates counterparty risk on collateral but gives easier access and better prices.

3.2 Collateral Liquidity Risk or "Margin Call Risk"

The widespread use of collateral to tackle counterparty exposure has given rise to one of the direst risks in derivatives trading: the risk of margin calls. Margin calls constitute a compelling reminder that risks may never be totally eradicated but reappear instead under a different form. Corporates, commercial banks, and financial institutions may fully hedge market risk with swaps; but market risk becomes credit risk on swap counterparties. Credit risk in swap may be mitigated with collateral, but credit risk morphs into the liquidity risk of margin calls.

3.2.1 A Short Analysis of the Margin Call Risk

Let us take the example of a commodity producer. Let us consider the case of a mining company selling gold and willing to hedge the price risk by selling forward so as to make its future revenues more predicTable. The firm has an OTC forward sales contract with a swap counterparty (see Fig. 12).

The value (MtM) at time t of the forward sale contract of one unit of gold for maturity T_1, started at time T_0, is valued as the cost of canceling the contract by entering into a forward purchase for the same maturity:

$$\frac{p_{T_o}^{T_1} - p_t^{T_1}}{(1 + r_t^{T_1})^{T_1 - t}}$$

With the notations:

$p_t^{T_1}$: Forward sell price at t of one ounce of gold for physical delivery at time T_1.

$p_{T_0}^{T_1}$: Forward sell price agreed in the T_1 forward gold sale contract agreed at T_0.

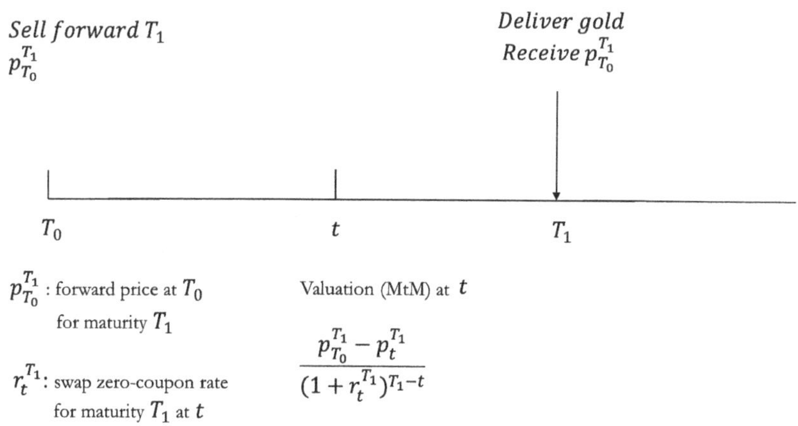

Fig. 12 Hedging strategy of a gold mining company (Ashanti)

$r_t^{T_1}$: Zero coupon swap rate for maturity T_1 taken at t.

The firm is producing gold so there is little doubt it will be able to honor the sales contract and deliver the physical gold on time at T_1. However, the forward contract—a derivative contract -, under the standard ISDA documentation, including the Credit Support Annex (CSA), requires the firm to post collateral if the MtM becomes negative. The MtM above can turn negative if the gold forward price at T_1 maturity goes above the contractual forward sale price agreed at T_0. If the gold forward price significantly rises, the gold producer may be asked to make a very substantial collateral payment. The producer may not have the cash to answer such a large and sudden margin call. Let us consider, for instance, the case of a large mining company selling forward a large amount of gold, 25 tons of gold (or about 729,175 oz given that 1 ton = 29,166.67 oz), at a forward price of 250 dollar per ounce. If the forward price of one ounce suddenly moves by 70 dollar to 320 dollar, the firm would have to answer a margin call representing $608 million (see Fig. 12).

This is a simplified calculation of what did happen to the Ghanaian gold producer Ashanti in 1999. The spot gold price did rise between mid-September and early October 1999 from $255 per ounce to $355 per ounce. Ashanti was faced with a $570 million loss in value in its hedging book and a $570 margin call for which it did not have the cash. Ashanti had to sell a 50% stake in one of its largest mines and issue warrants for 15% of its stock. Its stock price went down from $9.38 per share to $5.50 per share.

3.2.2 Margin Call Risk in the Recent History of Finance

Perhaps the most celebrated margin call case has been associated with Lehman Brothers. But looking at extensive investigations led on Lehman's downfall,[11] it appears that those margin calls which contributed to the bankruptcy were mostly those on the excessively large short-term repo financing position rather than those on derivatives: More haircut was applied on securities required as collateral by short-term repo lenders as Lehman's financial position was seen as weakening.

The case of Metallgesellschaft (in Box 2) probably remains the most dramatic example of how collateral calls in derivatives hedging can bring down an industrial giant, in that case one of the largest German industrial conglomerates in 1993.

Box 2: The case of Metallgesellschaft

Abundantly researched and documented,[12] the case of the German conglomerate Metallgesellschaft AG (MG), situated in the US energy sector, over 1991–1994, depicts the fatal consequences of an aggressive pricing business strategy, purportedly supported by derivatives hedging, and which ended up in a debacle precipitated by the margin calls.

MG's strategy was to expand its market share by offering energy supply contracts with prices fixed over the long term, while hedging the risk of rising energy prices with derivatives. The hedging, though, was hindered by two major flaws:

(i) The misalignment of the accounting rules: the one applying to the derivative hedge: Mark-to-Market (MtM) or fair value; and the one applying to the energy supply contracts, which differed from fair value (accrual accounting);
(ii) The underestimation of the risk of margin calls on derivative hedges.

In 1993, MG was among the 20 largest German companies, with 43,300 employees, 26 billion deutsche mark ($16 billion) in revenues and a strong position in the metal, mining and energy sectors encompassing engineering as well as trading and risk management services. Main shareholders included Dresdner Bank, Deutsche Bank, Allianz, Daimler and the Kuwait Investment Authority. The US subsidiary: Metallgesellschaft Refining and Marketing Inc. (MGRM), was distributing refined petroleum products to independent wholesalers and retailers. The MGRM's top executive, hired in 1991, had defined a strategy to expand MGRM's market share: offering protection to its clients against energy price volatility in its supply contracts by selling at a price fixed over a long horizon; MGRM would manage the risk in derivatives markets.

MGRM was offering its clients heating oil and gasoline supply contracts at a price fixed over a maturity of up to 10 years, while hedging the risk of a price increase in derivatives markets, either on the future exchange (NYMEX) or with OTC swaps. The price in the supply contract was set as the arithmetic average of the prices of the twelve NYMEX future contracts maturing within 12 months, plus a margin. Many of the supply contracts also included a sell-back option: the right to terminate the contract and receive in cash the Mark-to-Market.

As of September 1993, the outstanding supply contracts represented for MGRM an equivalent 154 millions of barrels exposure to a rise in heating oil and gasoline prices, a short position. MGRM's hedging strategy consisted in creating an equivalent long position in heating oil and gasoline derivatives. In a good delta hedge, MGRM's sensitivity to oil and gasoline prices in derivatives would offset that of the supply contracts. But the hedging strategy was not a perfect offset. Derivative hedges had a nominal equal to that of the supply contracts (160 million barrels) but were all short term: an estimated 55 million barrels in the NYMEX future contract maturing in the next month; about 110 million barrels in short dated swaps. Both short term derivative contracts were rolled over by MGRM. This had two implications:

1) There was a *basis risk*: movements in the curve of forward energy prices from 1 month to 10 years are not necessarily parallel shifts. If the long end were to increase while short term forward prices stayed constant, MGRM was not hedged.
2) More importantly, there was an *accounting mismatch*: the German accounting convention takes the less favorable of the two measures (MtM and accrual accounting), not allowing MGRM to book as revenues MtM gains in supply contracts should price decline; at the same time, MtM losses in the hedges would have to be recognized as losses, even if not realized as the derivative position was continuously rolled over.

The adverse scenario of an energy price decline materialized in 1993. As energy prices were falling throughout the year, MGRM was losing on its derivative positions. More crucially, MGRM was faced with increasingly large obligations to make collateral payments and margin calls. By the end of the summer, MGRM had used up all of its credit lines. Early December, as oil prices started to fall more rapidly, MGRM faced extreme difficulties to finance the margin calls required to continue to roll over its very large hedging position.

On December 6, MG publicly disclosed that its US subsidiary MGRM had lost over $1.5 billion on its energy hedges. MG quickly lost access to funding and transaction counterparties, and its share price fell by 13%. MG required $1 billion financing to honor its margin calls. On December 10, Deutsche Bank and Dresdner Bank agreed to a DM 1.5 billion loan; but on the same day, NYMEX requested higher margin calls, adding an over-collateral amount (or haircut) to the MtM. On December 17, the CEO and three members of MG's management board resigned. On December 28, NYMEX decided to impose limits on MGRM's total position in futures. At the same time, MGRM found it difficult to find counterparties on the swap OTC markets.

On January 1994, the new management of MG decided to put an end to MGRM's hedging and to realize losses, which stood at DM 1.97 billion for fiscal year 1992/1993. The new management arranged a bank bailout of $2.06 billion to save MG from bankruptcy (this would have been Germany's largest post WWII corporate bankruptcy). MG had another year of significant loss—DM 2.63 billion in fiscal year 1993/1994 but returned to break even in fiscal 1994/95. In mid-1995, MG was able to obtain DM 1.26 billion in new credit. Early 1996, MG had completely exited the US energy market and terminated all the fixed-price contract, but was still dealing with lawsuits associated with the MGRM fiasco.

Table 4 Margin calls and collateral posted by AIG. Source: Federal Reserve Bank of Chicago Working Paper 2014–2007

Date	*Margin*	*Collateral*
	Call ($bn)	*Posted ($bn)*
2008/6/30	15.8	13.2 g
2008/7/31	19.3	14.4
2008/9/12	23.4	18.9
2008/9/15	32.0	19.5
2008/9/16	33.8	22.4

Among the most traumatic moments of the 2008 crisis was the near-failure and the rescue, on September 16, 2008, of the American insurer AIG, a firm with $1 trillion in assets, rated AAA until March 2005. There is still debate whether AIG was a case of illiquidity of insolvency and if the rescue was justified. In any event, the cliff-effect AIG faced in its collateral posting obligations, on September 15, 2008, when it was downgraded from AA-/Aa3/AA- to A-/A2/A by S&P, Moody's and Fitch, resulted in AIG being unable to honor payments (see Table 4).

AIG had sold protection via CDS on a number of credit assets of various quality for a total notional of $527 billion as of end 2007 and had another 1.5 trillion in interest rate derivatives. AIG had ISDAs with a relatively small number of counterparties. Collateral to be posted by AIG was dependent on its rating. The downgrade on September 15, 2008, added $10 billion extra margin to be paid overnight. Table 4 shows collateral (or margin) due by AIG to all its derivatives counterparties and what was actually posted. Because CDS were sold on assets that were illiquid and difficult to value, there were frequent disputes between AIG and its counterparties (see Table 4).

4 An Enhanced Systemic Risk Mitigation Role

4.1 *The Status of Collateral in Post-2008 Regulation*

Post-2008 financial regulation targeted OTC derivatives in view of their opaqueness and their high potential for systemic disruption. The 2009 G20 summit in Pittsburgh outlined an agenda for financial market authorities to tackle the specific dangers of OTC derivatives, addressing counterparty credit risk, the contagion threat, and the opaqueness by centralizing clearing on Central Counterparties (CCPs).

The 2008 crisis had given bank regulators first-hand evidence of the shortcomings of collateral in OTC derivative markets. Standards of collateral posting in OTC derivatives markets were not robust enough to effectively protect entities and block the systemic risk transmission channel via the default of banks. Moreover, liquidity risk stemming from collateral posting—margin call risk—with its instant and potentially fatal effect, seemed to constitute another source of contagion in times of systemic stress.

At the Cannes Summit in November 2011, the G20 decided to add the strengthening of collateral posting—or margining—for uncleared OTC derivatives to the reform agenda.

All non-centrally cleared derivatives would receive a strong and direct incentive to migrate to CCPs via higher capital or margining requirements.

The final document: "Margin requirements for non-centrally cleared derivatives" was released in March 2015 by the Basel Committee on Banking Supervision (BCBS) and the Board of the International Organization of Securities Commissions (IOSCO).

The main recommendations have been implemented in the US regulation with the margining regulation published in December 2015 and coming into force in September 2016.[13] EU regulatory agencies are proceeding, as of November 2016, with the implementation of the margining regulation which should start early 2017.

Bank regulation had not focused so much on margining in the past. Lessons learned from the 2008 crisis have motivated regulation to significantly reinforce the well-established but also somehow incomplete margining practice of OTC derivatives markets. Relative to the comprehensive 2006 regulatory framework of Basel II, Basel III details many practical aspects of margining. The March 2015 Basel document: "*Margin requirements for non-centrally cleared derivatives*" extensively deals with the matter. The Basel document highlights the risk mitigation advantages of margining relative capital requirements: more targeted on the specific risk characteristics of a specific derivatives portfolio, more dynamic, more prone to convey incentives as it is the party creating exposure which has to support the mitigation cost.

Taking stock of the implementation of the post-2008 margining regulation for OTC derivatives, one can acknowledged ex post two effects: (i) encourage the migration of OTC derivative clearing to CCPs; (ii) but also, and this tends to become a long-lasting impact, codify, standardize and strengthen derivatives market practice with regard to margining. In doing so, regulatory authorities keep an eye on all the channels of transmission of systemic risk, and particularly liquidity. Margin call risk and the impact of collateral on the aggregate liquidity of capital markets are essential factors brought into the reform.

Key principles underlying the new regulation for uncleared derivatives margining are as follows:

- All financial firms and systematically important non-financial entities that engage in non-centrally cleared derivatives must exchange **initial and variation margin**;
- The methodology for calculating **initial and variation margin must reflect** both the **current exposure** (variation margin) and the **Potential Future Exposure** (initial margin), and ensure that exposures are covered with a high degree of confidence;
- Assets collected as collateral should be such that they can be liquidated in a reasonable amount of time to provide sufficient protection and should therefore be highly liquid assets or offer an appropriate haircut to ensure they can offer the desire value in times of market stress;
- **Initial margins should be exchanged among parties without netting of amounts; received collateral should be subject to arrangements (e.g., segregation) which fully protect the posting party against default.**

Consistent with the regulatory program of the G20 Pittsburgh and Cannes summits, the regulation of margin requirements for non-centrally cleared derivatives has two overarching objectives:

- Reduce systemic risk originating from non-centrally cleared derivatives, those derivatives that remain traded outside of the CCPs, the less prone to standardization and potentially the most illiquid, complex and opaque;
- Promote central clearing: Since CCPs require margining, so should non-cleared derivatives, but with even stronger collateral requirements since they have higher risk being outside of CCPs.

In the Basel March 2015 document, the BCBS and the IOSCO outline a timeline for phasing-in the new requirements on margining, which spans the September 1, 2016—September 1, 2020, time period, with, in general, smaller-sized market participants being given more time than large dealer banks and systematically important non-financial firms to implement. In subsequent paragraphs, we detail these reforms. We saw above that the USA is right on time, while the EU may have a lag of about a quarter.

So, the post-2008 agenda has been codified and has now been almost fully implemented. At least in a first round, we may add. As we noted in Chapter "Reshaping Derivatives Markets: The Post-2008 Ambition", there may be a pause in the reform process, as the first effects of the post-2008 regulation are being analyzed. In particular, the focus is presently on the systemic risk problem arising from the concentration of clearing in a small number of CCPs.

4.2 Reforms to Enhance Credit Protection

The March 2015 Basel document aims at making collateral deliver full and effective protection against counterparty risk in OTC derivatives trading, by systematically addressing prior shortcomings of collateral.

The first requirement is to make "*appropriate margining practices*" mandatory:

- For all OTC derivatives transactions that are not cleared on CCP, and
- For all entities that are key to the functioning of markets: financial firms and systematically important non-financial entities ("covered entities").[14]

The definition of the scope reflects the priority given to containing systemic risk as well as the cost of collateral management for smaller-sized market participants. For key market participants, the purpose is to no longer leave the margining practice dependent on bilateral contractual agreements. Margining practices must be standardized and fully cover the OTC derivatives markets.

4.2.1 Initial Margin for Replacement Risk and PFE

For all covered entities, the March 2015 Basel document requires to exchange not only variation margin but also initial margin in their non-centrally cleared derivatives transactions. This regulatory requirement will become mandatory in a phased-in manner as per the timeline in Fig. 13 (see Fig. 13).

The Basel document delineates quite clearly the purpose of variation margin and initial margin. Variation margin reflects current exposure, as measured by the Mark-to-Market. Initial margin reflects the Potential Future Exposure (PFE) over the Replacement Period. The initial margin requirement is explicitly introduced to protect against the Replacement Risk (see Sect. 3.1.1 above).

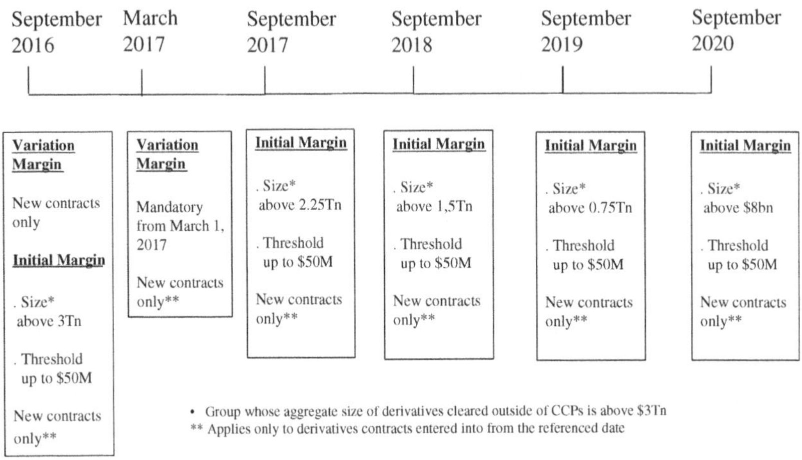

Fig. 13 Phase-in of new margining regulatory requirements

As a consequence, in order to offer effective protection, the initial margins posted by two counterparties cannot be netted.

The March 2015 Basel document further specifies that the PFE be computed as the maximum increase in MtM over a 10-business day period, at the 99% confidence level, using market data reflecting a significant financial stress.

While providing a standard formula for the calculation of the initial amount, Basel accepts internal models subject to their approval by the supervisory authority.

In the US, the Federal Reserve and the CFTC have set September 1, 2016, as the start date. Large swap dealers, to avoid disputes on the calculation of the initial margin, have agreed on a jointly developed open-source model called SIMM, which all of them recognize and use.

In the EU, the draft margining regulation for non-centrally cleared derivatives was published in March 2016 by the Joint Committee of European Supervisory Authorities (ESA, EBA, and EIOPA). At the time of this writing, it is still not final and is expected to become effective in the beginning of 2017.

4.2.2 Protecting the Value of the Collateral Received

The March 2015 Basel document insists on the resilience and the accessibility of collateral, particularly if the default of a large counterparty were to be accompanied by generalized market stress: "*assets collected as collateral should be highly liquid and should, after accounting for an appropriate haircut, be able to hold their value in a time of financial stress.*" Basel requirements also preconize haircuts and include a standardized haircut schedule: While cash (in the currency of the portfolio or in highly liquid currencies) has 0% haircut, a short maturity (less than one year) government bond would have a 0.5% haircut, and a short maturity corporate bond would have a 4% haircut.

Basel document also deals with the counterparty risk to which the entity posting collateral is exposed (see Sect. 3.1.2).

To provide effective protection, we saw that the initial margin should translate into a two-way flow—that is not netted—of payments among the two counterparties. For the same motive, the initial margin should be *segregated* (see Sect. 3.1.3) to be fully immune to the default event of the collateral receiving counterparty.

At the same time, the Basel Committee chose not to impose segregation on variation margins.

Let us note, however, that the segregation of the initial margin actually results in protecting the variation margin amount against the default of the receiving party. As we saw in Sect. 3.1.3., because the value of the posted collateral is equal to the negative MtM with the counterparty, the termination of this negative MtM would match the loss on the collateral, except if the MtM increases during the Replacement Period, and the surviving entity can be paid only a lesser amount to replace. In Sect. 3.1.3., we concluded this situation risk—having the negative MtM become smaller, in absolute value, than the posted collateral, and having this excess in posted collateral becoming an exposure to the counterparty—was similar to the Credit Risk exposure during the Replacement Period and could be measured as a PFE. Consequently, the initial margin provides all the needed protection.

4.2.3 Dealing with Liquidity Risk Aspects

A. Margin Call Risk

The December 2010 Basel III reference document[15] constitutes a compendium of post-2008 regulation. It also instructs banks to set up a policy for managing Margin Call risk:

A bank employing the internal models method must ensure that its cash management policies account simultaneously for the liquidity risks of potential incoming margin calls in the context of exchanges of variation margin or other margin types, such as initial or independent margin, under adverse market shocks, potential incoming calls for the return of excess collateral posted by counterparties, and calls resulting from a potential downgrade of its own public rating.

B. The trade-off Liquidity versus Protection

The March 2015 Basel paper dealing with margining contains several provisions aimed at preserving the liquidity in derivatives and capital markets.

Regulators are aware that strict requirements, quite desirable from a counterparty risk mitigation point of view, such as the high quality of assets eligible as collateral, or the segregation (and absence of re-hypothecation) of posted collateral) could have unintended and undesirable effects. Re-hypothecation (see Sect. 3.1.3 above) allows derivatives markets to function with the same asset base. Segregation could result in having most of the assets eligible for collateral "trapped" in segregated collateral accounts and no longer available. This is why Basel limits the obligation of segregation to initial margins while variation margin securities can be re-hypothecated.

In the same vein, Basel regulators have allowed for a broad range of assets eligible as collateral, including corporate bonds, asset-backed securities, equities, and gold. The quality requirement is managed through the haircut adjustment.

Notes

1. Notice that the MtM here does not reflect the valuation of default risk in this paragraph; this means in particular that the value of the MtM, with cash flows discounted using a default-risk free yield curve, will be the same for counterparties A and B but with opposite signs.
2. At this initial conceptual stage, we ignore notions such as that of *Threshold*, which result in having, under certain conditions, collateral being less than the MtM. We also ignore, at the moment, the notion of *Initial Margin*.
3. The ISDA was comprised of above 800 members in 2014, including end-users (42%), derivative dealers (24%), and service providers (34%). Banks

represent the largest group among members (30%), followed by law firms (24%), asset managers (10%), and government entities (10%). Large global investment banks (JP Morgan, Goldman Sachs, Bank of America Merrill Lynch, Citibank, Morgan Stanley, Deutsche Bank, Barclays, HSBC, UBS, Credit Suisse, BNP Paribas, Societe Generale…) and large asset managers such as Blackrock or PIMCO would sit on the ISDA Board (ISDA 2014).

4. There are in fact two versions of the standard ISDA CSA. One which applies New York law (collateral is pledged); one which applies English law (dated 1995, where there is a title transfer on posted collateral).
5. During the 2007-2008, haircuts on collateral posted by investment banks in their short-term securitized wholesale funding operations (repos) played a particular role in the deterioration of their liquidity position. Since then, several analyses have attempted at understanding the role played by haircuts. A 2015 Federal Reserve Board paper by Sebastian Infante explores to what extent dealer banks may benefit from a liquidity windfall by receiving collateral from weaker counterparties (in derivatives and repos) such as hedge funds on which they apply larger haircuts than those they agree with counterparties to which they would post collateral.
6. Source: ISDA Margin Survey 2014 (ISDA 2014).
7. The party having posted securities as collateral has the right to require certain securities returned for specific use. If the collateral receiving party cannot return the very security being requested, it may return instead an equivalent security, having equivalent risk and liquidity features. In fact, according to the ISDA, most CSAs do not permit the return of an equivalent security. If the secured party (pledgee) is not able to deliver it on the day of the request, an equivalent could be used temporarily while the pledgee is acquiring it.
8. Manhoman Singh, Velocity of Pledged Collateral: Analysis and Implications, IMF Working Paper, Nov 2011 (Singh 2011).
9. The ISDA noted that, in the bankruptcy of Lehman, many investors had been exposed to significant losses due to the payment of IA while giving Lehman the right to re-hypothecate the IA. IAs were not segregated and had been freely used by Lehman. Claims on IAs were treated as general unsecured claims.
10. The reader interest by this aspect can read the analyses of Mahmohan Singh or Gary Gorton.
11. US Bankruptcy Court Southern District of New York, Chapter 11 Case No 0813555 (JMP), Report of Anton R. Valukas, Examiner (US Bankruptcy Court, New York 2010).
12. This case study uses the author's own market sources and the following papers and analysis: Allen B. Frankel and David E. Palmer; John

Digenan, The case of financial risks at German non-financial firms: the case of Metallgesellschaft, Board of Governors of the Federal System, International Finance Discussion Papers, August 1996 (Frankel & Palmer 1996); Dan Felson, Robert Kelly and Ann Wiemert, PRMIA.org; Antonio S. Mello and John E. Parsons, Journal of Applied Corporate Finance, Spring 1995; Franklin R. Edwards: The case of Metallgesellschaft, Derivatives Quarterly, Spring 1995 (Edwards 1995); Metallgesellschaft AG History, International Directory of Company Histories, Vol 16. St James Press, 1997.

13. The US CFTC (Commodity Futures Trading Commission), the agency regulating swap markets, approved the Final Rule on Margin Requirements for Uncleared Swaps for Swap Dealers and Major Swap Participants on December 15, 2016. Largest participants had to comply with the rule from September 1, 2016.
14. Sovereigns, central banks and multilateral development banks are also explicitly exempt from mandatory margining in the March 2015 BCBS IOSCO document.
15. Basel III: A global regulatory framework for more resilient banks and banking systems - December 2010 (rev June 2011).

References

ISDA. (2006). *Margin survey 2006.*

ISDA. (2010, March). *Market review of OTC derivative bilateral collateralization practices.*

ISDA. (2014, April). *ISDA margin survey 2014.*

ISDA. (2014, October 20). *ISDA response to IOSCO consultation on risk mitigation standards for non-centrally cleared OTC derivatives.*

ISDA. (2014, April). *Size and uses of the non-cleared derivatives market.*

Singh, M. (2011). *Velocity of pledged collateral.* IMF Working Paper WP/11/256.

US Bankruptcy Court, New York. (2010). Report of Anton R. Valukas, Lehman Brothers Holdings, Chapter 11 Case No 08-13555.

Adjusting for Credit and Debt Value: CVA and DVA

Abstract Chapter 4 presents the CVA and DVA adjustments reflecting in the market value of a derivative or a portfolio of derivatives the expected cost of the counterparty's default (CVA) and, symmetrically, the expected benefit of one's own default (DVA). The Chapter presents formulae for the CVA and DVA metrics, with or without collateral posting, with or without credit risk on collateral posted. The Chapter presents formulae that relate the CVA and DVA to the credit spreads of the two counterparties to a portfolio of derivatives. The last section provides a proof of these formulae in a canonic continuous-time, risk neutral derivative market framework.

Keywords Bilateral adjustment · Credit spread · CVA credit value adjustment formula · Defaultable bond/swap · DVA debt value adjustment formula · EAD exposure at default · EE expected exposure · ENE expected negative exposure · EPE expected positive exposure · Financial firms LGD loss given default · PD probability of default · Replacement risk Risk neutral valuation · RR recovery rate · Systematically important Non-Financial firms

I. Zelenko, *Credit Risk Management for Derivatives*,
DOI 10.1007/978-3-319-57975-7_4

1 Credit Value Adjustment: CVA

The concept of credit value adjustment (CVA) appeared in derivatives markets in the beginning of the 2000 decade. Its use then expanded and gradually went beyond cutting-edge derivative houses. Then, given the role played by derivatives counterparty credit risk (CCR) during the 2007-08 crisis, and particularly by the potentially devastating impact of possible very rapid shifts in the CVA component of the Mark-to-Market (MtM) of a swap or derivative book, regulatory authorities started to give CVA their utmost attention. One of the key changes in the post-2008 regulation has been the introduction of a new CVA capital requirement. The first version, in December 2010, of the new Basel III compendium of rules included, together with an expanded counterparty credit risk section, the introduction of a new capital charge for banks to deal with the risk posed by the changes in the CVA of the derivatives position.

In this paragraph, we first present key themes guiding the understanding and use of the CVA. We then outline a practical calculation formula, with reference to a more detailed analysis, underpinned by financial theory foundations, in paragraph 3. We then proceed with analyzing how the CVA can be employed.

1.1 CVA: Definition and Overview

The CVA is the valuation of counterparty credit risk. In the pricing of a derivative, the CVA is the component which compensates for the potential default of the counterparty. The CVA is the expectation of the loss due to default, computed over the remaining life of the derivative contract.

The CVA is firstly defined for a derivative contract taken in isolation but it is mainly used, measured, and monitored at the level of the entire derivative portfolio. The CVA is computed on a *Netting Set* covered by an ISDA with a derivative counterparty, and by a CSA agreement specifying the collateral requirements. But the CVA also enters into the pricing of all new derivative trades entering into the Netting Set. Even when computing the CVA at portfolio's level, the CVA has first to be estimated separately for each of the derivatives in the portfolio before being aggregated.

The CVA is part of the derivative's pricing. Consequently, it is calculated with the same risk neutral probability that applies to the pricing of the derivative. The CVA offers the remarkable property of being separated from the risk neutral pricing of the derivative (see paragraph 3 for details on the formal expression of the CVA). This means that the value (MtM) of a portfolio of derivatives, a Netting Set among entities A and B, is equal to the sum of its risk neutral valuation and its CVA. The value of the portfolio, seen from A's point of view, is:

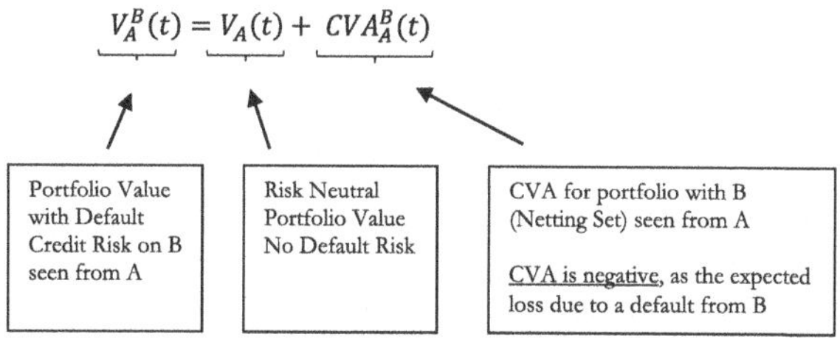

The CVA is trade, portfolio, and counterparty-specific. The CVA reflects the characteristics of every trade the portfolio; it reflects the characteristics of the portfolio—the Netting Set, and how the derivatives' sensitivities to market variables can match and offset each other within this Netting Set; and, perhaps most essentially, the CVA reflects the credit quality of the counterparty. As such, the CVA calculation will include the following:

- The Probability of Default (PD) of the counterparty;
- The Exposure at Default (EAD) projected over the life of the portfolio, then discounted and aggregated as an expectation;
- The Recovery Rate (RR), or equivalently the Loss Given Default (LGD).

In its calculation, the CVA reflects the protection offered by the posting of collateral over the Netting Set, as described in the CSA of the ISDA contract. Therefore, the EAD entering into the CVA calculation is the residual exposure, the part which is not covered by collateral, and which is the sum of:

- The part of the MtM which is not collateralized, either because the counterparty is not posting collateral, or as a result of the Threshold and Minimum Transfer Amount clauses in the CSA (see also Chapter 3 on collateral);
- The Replacement Risk, measured as expectation of the future exposure over the Replacement Period;

When estimating the CVA, Replacement Risk is calculated as the average deviation over the Replacement Period, not as the maximum deviation (at the 99% confidence level), contrary to the PFE which measures a worst-case exposure for counterparty risk management purposes. As a valuation, a pricing metrics, the CVA uses the expected value.

We note $EE_A^B(t_i)$ the expected discounted exposure of A to B, or the expectation of the discounted value of the portfolio at t_i from the point of view of A. The *Expected Exposure* (EE) is always a positive number, like the PFE. If the expected value at a future point in time is negative, this would not count as an exposure in the CVA calculation. In order to distinguish, we will note it NEE: *Negative Expected Exposure* so that *Expected Exposure* is positive or null. The Expected Exposure reflects the protection offered by collateral through the CSA of the ISDA. It may also reflect the expected effect of protections against default of B acquired by A, either via Credit Default Swap (CDS) or via other forms of credit enhancement. Figure 1 below depicts what could be the evolution of the Expected Exposure over time, mapped on a grid of successive time points t_i which are going to be used to derive a practical formula for the CVA (see Fig. 1)

When first estimating the CVA at instrument's level, and looking at the three variables driving the CVA: (i) PD: Probability of Default; (ii) EAD: Expected Exposure at Default; and (iii) RR: Recovery Rate. The Expected Exposure will use as input a series of points EE_{Ai} over the maturity of the derivatives' portfolio; the Probability of Default will also depend on the time horizon; however, the recovery rate will be assumed constant.

1.2 CVA Formula

1.2.1 CVA Formula with Probabilities of Default

We are now ready to present the CVA formula (for full derivation see paragraph 3 of this chapter)

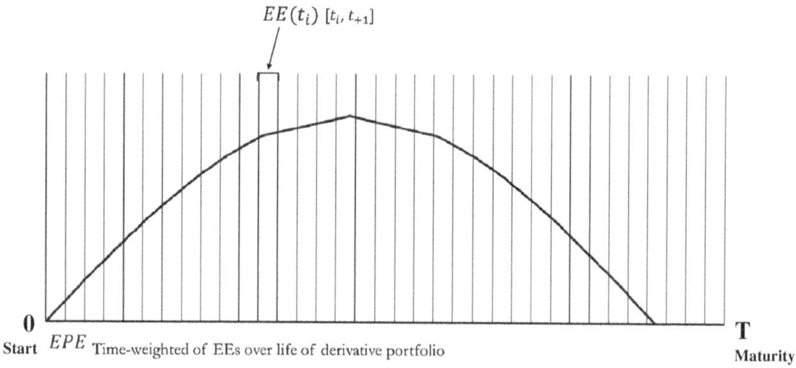

Fig. 1 Evolution of the evolution of Expected Exposure over the life of a portfolio

$$CVA_A^B(t) = -(1 - R_B) \sum_{t_i=t}^{T-1} PD_B(t_i, t_{i+1}) EE_A^B(t_i) \tag{I}$$

With:

CVA_A^B:	CVA on a portfolio of derivatives or Netting Set between trading counterparts A and B, calculated from the point of view of A, with Credit (e.g. default risk) Value Adjustment on B
R_B:	*Recovery rate* on a default on derivatives in the portfolio with counterparty B; the alternative notation is the Loss Given Default (or LGD)
LGD_B	Loss Given Default on entity B; $LGD_B = (1 - R_B)$
$PD_B(t_i, t_{i+1})$:	Probability of Default of B in the future, in the time interval (see Fig. 1): $[t_i, t_{i+1}]$;
$EE_A^B(t_i)$:	Expected Exposure of A to B at the future time t_i, computed for all derivatives in the Netting Set, and present-valued at time t;
T:	Maturity of the portfolio, i.e., maturity of the instrument with the longest tenor in the Netting Set

The Expected Exposure is a positive number. In this first paragraph, we only assume that the Expected Exposure reflects the protection offered by collateral through the CSA of the ISDA and the protections against default of B acquired by A. We do not detail yet the mechanism of collateral.

The computation-intensive part of the calculation resides in the proper estimate of the discounted expected values of the Expected Exposure. Recovery Rates, obtained from rating agencies data, can be fine-tuned by an institution based on its own risk experience or knowledge of recovery processes.

1.2.2 CVA Formula with Credit Spreads

Probabilities of default for several maturity points in the future can also be obtained from the three major rating agencies: Standard & Poor's (S&P), Moody's, and Fitch. Alternatively, probabilities of default can be derived from the CDS or bond spreads quoted in the market for the counterparty B. If sourced from the market, the probabilities of default would reflect the volatility in CDS and bond spreads. In that case, the user may prefer the equivalent CVA formula below explicitly showing the influence of the market credit spread of B (see paragraph 3 for the derivation).

$$CVA_A^B(t) = -LGD_B \sum_{t_i=t}^{T-1} [e^{-\frac{s_{B,t}^{t_i}}{LGD_B}(t_i-t)} - e^{-\frac{s_{B,t}^{t_{i+1}}}{LGD_B}(t_{i+1}-t)}] EE_A^B(t_i) \qquad \text{(II)}$$

With:

$s_{B,t}^{t_i}$: The credit spread at time t of the entity B at the horizon t_i.

Spreads are the numbers expressed in percentage points or basis points. If we take a first-order approximation of the expression in (II), and replace the discounted expected exposure numbers by their time average: the discounted Expected Positive Exposure (EPE, which is the loan exposure equivalent of the derivative) we see a shorter and more intuitive "face" of the CVA appearing:

$$CVA_A^B(t) \cong -s_{B,t}^{t,T} EPE_A^B(t) \qquad \text{(III)}$$

With:

$EPE_A^B(t)$: Discounted Expected Positive Exposure
$s_{B,t}^{t,T}$: Average credit spread of B taken over maturity bucket $[t, T]$ taken at time t

Under the form in (III), we are easily reminded that the CVA is, in essence, a credit spread time the expected exposure on counterparty.

1.3 CVA Formula with Collateral

Under an ISDA contract with a Credit Support Annex (CSA)-governing collateral posting, the Expected Exposure is determined, at the time of default, by:

- The uncollateralized exposure, mainly defined by the *Threshold* in the CSA, and, but to a much lesser extent by the *Minimum Transfer Amount* (see Chapter on Collateral);
- The expected increase in the MtM, over the posted collateral, during the *Replacement Period*;
- And maybe the *Independent Amount* (IA), in the case counterparty B had been downgraded prior to default to a rating (usually BBB + or BBB) triggering the IA in the CSA; in that case, if the IA was well defined in the CSA so as to provide adequate protection against the maximum potential increase in MtM during the Replacement Period, the Expected Exposure should always be equal to zero at all future dates.

We now give a formulation for the CVA in the presence of collateral[1]. The difficulty resides in the proper estimate of the future values of the expected potential loss should there be a default: $EE_A^B(t_i)$.

$$CVA_A^B(t) = -LGD_B \sum_{t_i=t}^{T-1} PD_B(t_i, t_{i+1}) EE_A^B(t_i) \qquad \text{(III)}$$

With:

For Financial Firms and Systematically Important Non-Financial Firms), and knowing that the new Basel regulation on collateral imposes an Initial Margin to protect against the Replacement Risk on default:

$$EE_A^B(t_i) = \mathbb{E}_t\left[D(t,t_i)\{\underbrace{\mathbb{1}_{\{0\le PV_A^B(t_i)\le H\}}PV_A^B(t_i)}_{\text{Exposure below Threshold Positive Mark to Market of Portfolio}} + \underbrace{\mathbb{1}_{\{H<PV_A^B(t_i)\}}H\}}_{\text{Exposure above Threshold is equal to Threshold}}\right] \quad \text{(IV)}$$

For other entities:

$$EE_A^B(t_i) = \mathbb{E}_t\left[D(t,t_i)\{\underbrace{\mathbb{1}_{\{0\le PV_A^B(t_i)\le H\}}\left(PV_A^B(t_i) + \frac{\Delta^+PV_A^B(t_i)}{LGD_B}\right)}_{\text{Exposure below Threshold is the Positive Mark to Market of Portfolio plus the change in the market value over the Replacement Period}} + \underbrace{\mathbb{1}_{\{H<PV_A^B(t_i)\}}\left(H + \frac{\Delta^+PV_A^B(t_i)}{LGD_B}\right)\}}_{\text{Exposure above Threshold is equal to Threshold plus the change in the market value over the Replacement Period}}\right] \quad \text{(V)}$$

With additional notations;

PV_A^B: Value (or Mark-to-Market) of the derivatives portfolio (or Netting Set) between A and B, measured from A's point of view, and reflecting the default risk of B.

H: Threshold for collateral posting in the CSA: counterparts do not post-collateral when the MtM is below H.

$1_{\{event\}}$: Indicator function, which takes the value 1 when the event is realized or 0 otherwise.

$\Delta^+PV_A^B$: the variation, if positive, of PV_A^B over the Replacement Period

Note that the change in Mark-to-Market of the portfolio over the Replacement Period is not an exposure to B for the entity A. It is a pure market risk at this stage and the Loss Given Default on B which applies to the whole $CVA_A^B(t)$ calculation does not apply to $\Delta^+PV_A^B$. This is why it is divided by LGD_B in expression (V).

1.4 CVA Formula with Credit Risk on Collateral

We now provide the most complete CVA formula in the situation where counterparts A and B have agreed to an ISDA contract with a CSA and see the collateral they post as also being exposed to the default of the

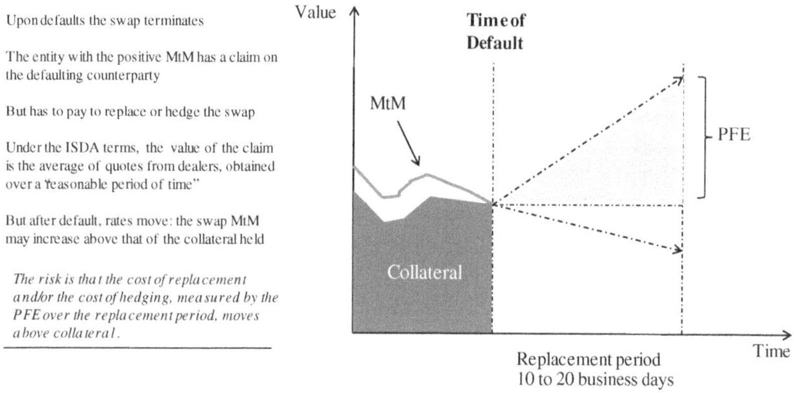

Fig. 2 Key elements of CVA calculation with collateral

other counterparty. In this paragraph, we will reflect the March 2015 Basel document on the regulation of margining practices for OTC derivatives. With the posting of Initial Margin among covered entities, the Basel Committee has introduced a fundamental change in its post-crisis attempt to strengthen the effectiveness of collateral as a means to make derivatives truly default-risk free (see Fig. 2 (AQ: Figure 2 was not cited in the text so a citation has been inserted. Please provide a correction if this is inaccurate.)). The protection provided by this Initial Margin against the default of the receiving entities (pledgee), through the obligation to segregate this margin and make it primarily accessible to the posting entity (pledgor) is also a major regulatory change. However, with the intention to foster the liquidity of the market and the ability of collateral, the Basel regulator decided to this new segregation clause would only apply to the Initial Margin. The Basel Committee did not change the pre-2008 market collateral re-hypothecation practice on variation margins. Moreover, these new regulatory clauses—Initial Margin and segregated account—only apply to "covered entities," that is, the financial firms and systematically important non-financial firms. On this topic, the reader may also refer to Chapter 3 on Collateral.

We consider that entity A has a negative MtM, has posted collateral, and B is in default. According to the CSA, the claim of the surviving entity is an average of quotes received from swap dealers during a "reasonable period of time" after the time of default. If, during this period,

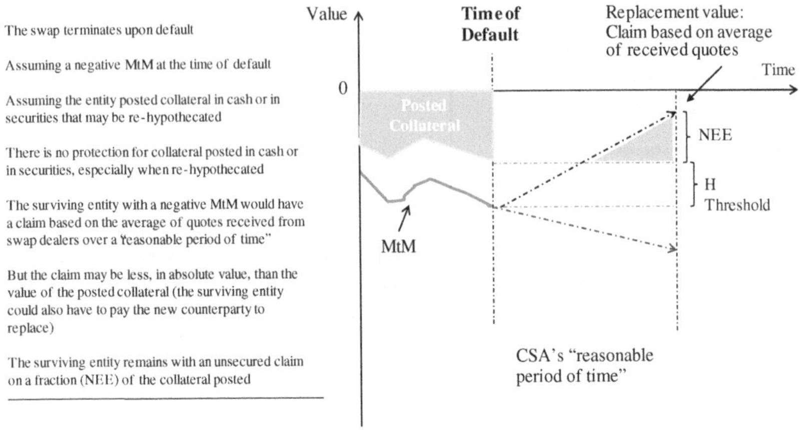

Fig. 3 CVA calculation: Negative Expected Exposure on posted collateral

the MtM increases so that the amount of collateral posted by the surviving entity is in excess of the absolute value of the negative MtM (see Fig. 3), and if the collateral cannot be retrieved (in particular, if it has been re-hypothecated) the surviving entity ends up with an exposure (which will be measured as a Negative Expected Exposure under the conventions used for measuring counterparty credit risk), and a claim equal to this excess collateral. If the two counterparties were "covered entities," this claim would be covered by the Initial Margin (immune to default via the segregation). But this is not the case for "non-covered entities."

The final formula we present integrates this aspect. It is, therefore, the most complete. Since we now include cases when, at a present or future time, an entity has a negative exposure, we introduce in our calculations the notation:

$NEE_A^B(t_i)$: Negative Expected Exposure of A to B at time t_i, computed for all derivatives in the Netting Set; the NEE is a negative number.

$$CVA_A^B(t) = -LGD_B \sum_{t_i=t}^{T-1} PD_B(t_i, t_{i+1}) \left[EE_A^B(t_i) - NEE_A^B(t_i) \right] \qquad \text{(VI)}$$

With: - the discounted Expected Exposure term $EE_A^B(t_i)$ similar to the previous formula without default risk on collateral, with two versions: one for Basel covered entities and one for non-covered entities;
- the additional discounted Negative Expected Exposure $NEE_A^B(t_i)$ reflecting the risk on posted collateral.

$$EE_A^B(t_i) = \mathbb{E}_t\left[D(t,t_i)\{1_{\{0\leq PV_A^B(t_i)\leq H\}}PV_A^B(t_i) + 1_{\{H<PV_A^B(t_i)\}}H\}\right] \quad \text{(IV)}$$

For Basel covered entities

And for non-covered entities:

$$EE_A^B(t_i) = \mathbb{E}_t\Bigg[D(t,t_i)\{1_{\{0\leq PV_A^B(t_i)\leq H\}}(PV_A^B(t_i) + \frac{\Delta^+ PV_A^B(t_i)}{LGD_B}) + 1_{\{H<PV_A^B(t_i)\}}\left(H + \frac{\Delta^+ PV_A^B(t_i)}{LGD_B}\right)\}\Bigg] \quad \text{(VII)}$$

$$-NEE_A^B(t_i) = \mathbb{E}_t\left[D(t,t_i)\{\Delta^+ PV_A^B(t_i) - H\}1_{\{PV_A^B(t_i)<-H\}}\right] \quad \text{(VIII)}$$

2 DVA and Bilateral Adjustment

The concept of DVA is fully consistent with the one of CVA. It is an adjustment of the value of a derivative to reflect the possibility of one's own default before the contract matures. It is a default-risk adjusted adjustment to the derivative's valuation. But while being consistent with the CVA, there is something very counterintuitive in the notion of DVA, and even, one may argue, something paradoxical.

2.1 DVA: Definition and Overview

The DVA measures the gain a party to a derivative contract may make if it were to default before the contract matures.

The gain simply reflects the fact that, in a very realistic manner, the defaulting counterparty would not pay the full value in case it has a negative exposure at the time of default, but only a fraction of it (customarily measured by the recovery rate).

One of the paradoxes of the DVA is that, for a derivative market participant that includes the DVA in the valuation of its derivative portfolio, deterioration in its credit quality, an increase in its probability of default, or a drop in its own recovery rate, pushes up the value of the DVA and increases the value of its portfolio.

Another counterintuitive implication of the DVA can be seen when contemplating the very possibility of default: for the counterparty in default, what would be the advantage of having maximized its DVA if it is bankrupt.

Like for the CVA, the DVA is first defined for a separate derivative but its main use is at the level of the entire derivative portfolio between two counterparties A and B, the Netting Set.

Like the CVA, the DVA possesses the interesting property of being additive. The single derivative or the portfolio of derivatives is valued in a classic risk neutral and default-risk-free setup. Then, just as the CVA can be added to adjust for the default of the counterparty (counterparty B if we take the point of view of A), the DVA can also be added to reflect the value embedded in A's own potential default.

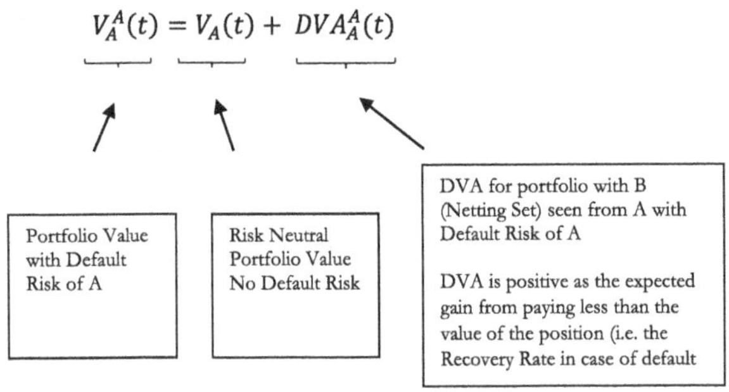

2.2 *DVA Formula*

2.2.1 DVA Formula with Probabilities of Default

The DVA formula is very similar to the CVA formula. The full derivation can be found in paragraph 3.

$$DVA_A^A(t) = -LGD_A \sum_{t_i=t}^{T-1} PD_A(t_i, t_{i+1}) NEE_A^A(t_i) \qquad \text{(IX)}$$

With the notations:

DVA_A^A: DVA on a portfolio of derivatives or Netting Set between trading counterparts A and B, calculated from the point of view of A (subscript), with Debt (or default risk) Value Adjustment on A (superscript)

R_A: *Recovery rate* on a default on derivatives in the portfolio with counterparty A; the alternative notation is the Loss Given Default (or LGD)

LGD_A Loss Given Default on entity A; $LGD_A = (1 - R_A)$

$PD_A(t_i, t_{i+1})$: Probability of Default of A in the future, in the time interval (see Fig. 1): $[t_i, t_{i+1}]$;

$NEE_A^A(t_i)$: Negative Expected Exposure of A to B, that is with default risk on A (superscript) at the future time t_i, computed for all derivatives in the Netting Set;

T: Maturity of the portfolio, i.e., maturity of the instrument with the longest tenor in the Netting Set

The Negative Expected Exposure is a negative number. Under an ISDA contract with a CSA applying to the Netting Set, the Negative Expected Exposure will incorporate the effects of collateral. In what follows, we will gradually introduce this aspect.

2.2.2 DVA Formula with Credit Spreads

The probability of default of A is reflecting in the credit spreads embedded in bonds issued by A or Credit Default Swaps providing default protection on A.

$$DVA_A^A(t) = -LGD_A \sum_{t_i=t}^{T-1} [e^{-\frac{s_{A,t}^{t_i}}{LGD_A}(t_i - t)} - e^{-\frac{s_{A,t}^{t_{i+1}}}{LGD_A}(t_{i+1} - t)}] NEE_A^A(t_i) \quad \text{(X)}$$

With:

$s_{A,t}^{t_i}$: credit spread of A at time t for the horizon t_i.

Like for the CVA, if we take a first-order approximation of the exponential functions and if we replace the discounted negative expected exposure numbers by their time average: the Expected Negative Exposure (ENE), we can derive the following simple intuitive approximate DVA formula (note that ENE is negative in formula (XI)):

$$DVA_A^A(t) \cong -s_{A,t}^{t,T} ENE_A^A(t) \quad \text{(XI)}$$

2.3 DVA Formula with Collateral

As was done for the CVA in paragraph 1.3., we now introduce the protection provided by the collateral into the estimate of the DVA. The Threshold and the Minimum Transfer Amount clauses in the CSA create fractions of the Mark-to-Market that are not collateralized. From a DVA point of view, these uncollateralized exposures will be directly reflected in the Negative Expected Exposure (NEE). There is a perfect symmetry with the CVA calculation in that case. The uncollateralized part of the NEE, of which only the recovery rate will be eventually paid by the defaulting entity to its counterparty, generates a gain, included in the DVA estimate, in case of default.

We also consider that the other main component of the Expected Exposure in the CVA calculation, consisting in the potential increase in the MtM during the replacement period, is matched by an equivalent in the DVA calculation. As per the ISDA terms, the value of the claim for the surviving entity is equal to the average of quotes received from swap dealers over "a reasonable period of time." So the Negative Expected Exposure will include the variation in the MtM in a way similar to the CVA. There is a difference, however, in the calculation. In the CVA calculation, the potential uncollateralized increase of the MtM is measured by a 10-day or a 20-day expected increase in MtM, in line with regulation. In the DVA, it is the reverse: the potential increase in the Negative Expected Exposure is also the expected change over a number of days. The number of days will be subject to the legal interpretation of "a reasonable period of time" for the surviving counterparty to receive quotes.

Similar to CVA calculations in paragraph 1.3 above, the new Basel regulation on initial margining opens two cases in the DVA calculation. The additional exposure due to the increase in the MtM after default, whose maximum amount is estimated by the PFE, will be covered by the Initial Margin. The Initial Margin has the status of segregated collateral (see Chapter 3 on collateral) and the defaulting entity cannot default on it. So there is no DVA gain for counterparties that are "covered entities" in the sense of this regulation.

The DVA formula in the presence of collateral is:

$$DVA_A^A(t) = -LGD_A \sum_{t_i=t}^{T-1} PD_A(t_i, t_{i+1}) NEE_A^A(t_i) \qquad \text{(XI)}$$

With the Negative Exposure being equal to:

For "entities non-covered" by the Basel regulation on margining:

$$DVA_A^A(t) = -LGD_A \sum_{t_i=t}^{T-1} PD_A(t_i,t_{i+1})\,\mathbb{E}_t\Big[D(t,t_i)\{\underbrace{\mathbb{1}_{\{0\geq PV_A^A(t_i)\geq -H\}}(PV_A^A(t_i)+\Delta^- PV_A^A(t_i))}_{\text{If MtM within Threshold H, the Negative Expected Exposure is equal to MtM plus the negative variation over a reasonable "period of time"}} + \underbrace{\mathbb{1}_{\{-H>PV_A^A(t_i)\}}(-H+\Delta^- PV_A^A(t_i))}_{\text{If MtM is beyond Threshold the NEE is equal to: Threshold plus the negative variation over a "reasonable period of time"}}\}\Big] \quad \text{(XII)}$$

For entities that are "covered" by the Basel margining regulation (financial firms and systematically important non-financial firms):

$$DVA_A^A(t) = -LGD_A \sum_{t_i=t}^{T-1} PD_A(t_i,t_{i+1})\,\mathbb{E}_t\Big[D(t,t_i)\{\underbrace{\mathbb{1}_{\{0\geq PV_A^A(t_i)\geq -H\}}PV_A^A(t_i)}_{\text{If MtM within Threshold H, the Negative Expected Exposure is equal to MtM}} - \underbrace{\mathbb{1}_{\{-H>PV_A^A(t_i)\}}H}_{\text{If MtM is beyond Threshold the NEE is equal to Threshold}}\}\Big] \quad \text{(XIII)}$$

2.4 DVA Formula with Credit Risk on Collateral

What would be the consequence for DVA calculations of considering the default risk on collateral and is there any symmetry with the CVA case? In paragraph 1.4, where we presented the most complete formula for the CVA, including risk of default on posted collateral, we assessed the risk in the following way:

If A, with negative MtM, has posted collateral to B in default. Based on the CSA, the claim of A is an average of quotes received from swap dealers during a "reasonable period of time" after the time of default. If, during this period, the MtM increases so that the amount of collateral posted by A is in excess of the absolute value of the negative MtM, and if the collateral cannot be retrieved, A ends up with an exposure (a Negative Expected Exposure), and a claim equal to this excess collateral. If the two counterparties were "covered entities," this claim would be covered by the Initial Margin (immune to default via *the segregation). But this is not the case for "non-covered entities."*

We now consider the same situation from the DVA's side. A has received collateral but may not give it back in full if in default, which could be seen

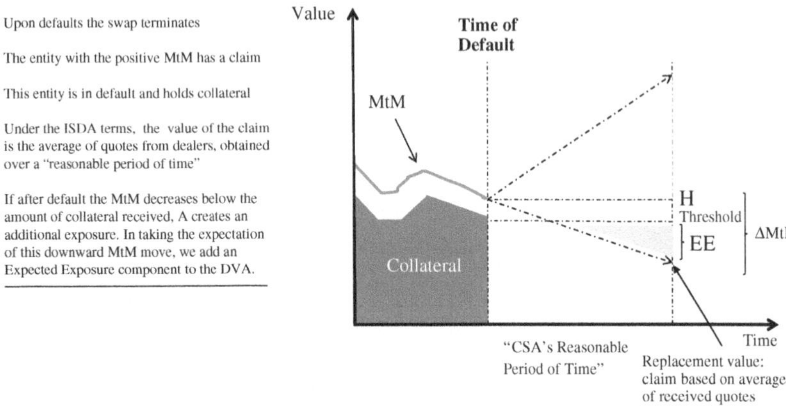

Fig. 4 DVA calculation: Expected Exposure on received collateral

as a gain. As in the CVA analysis, one has to remember that the collateral posted to the defaulting counterparty was representing a positive MtM for the defaulting counterparty. Keeping the collateral may be considered as revenue but, in fact, the surviving counterparty will not make the payment associated with the termination of the swap as long as the collateral is not given back. So there is no net gain for the defaulting counterparty, assuming there is no change in MtM in the period immediately after default.

We assume A has a positive MtM and holds collateral. If the MtM, seen from A's point of view, were to decrease, A would then hold collateral in excess and one could consider this excess collateral as part of the expected exposure to A. Under the notations we have been using for CCR, seen from A, the expected value of this amount would be an Expected Exposure, see (see Fig. 4).

We can now present the most complete formula for the DVA.

$$DVA_A^A(t) = -LGD_A \sum_{t_i=t}^{T-1} PD_A(t_i, t_{i+1}) \left[NEE_A^A(t_i) - EE_B^A(t_i) \right] \quad \text{(XIV)}$$

With the discounted Expected Exposure term $EE_B^A(t_i)$ reflects credit risk on posted collateral and:

$$NEE_A^A(t_i) = \mathbb{E}_t \Big[D(t, t_i) \{ 1_{\{0 \geq PV_A^A(t_i) \geq -H\}} PV_A^A(t_i) - 1_{\{-H > PV_A^A(t_i)\}} H \} \Big] \quad \text{(XV)}$$

For Basel covered entities

And for non-covered entities:

$$\begin{aligned} NEE_A^A(t_i) =& \mathbb{E}_t\Big[D(t,t_i)\{1_{\{0\geq PV_A^A(t_i)\geq -H\}}(PV_A^A(t_i)+\Delta^- PV_A^A(t_i)) \\ &+1_{\{-H>PV_A^A(t_i)\}}(-H+\Delta^- PV_A^A(t_i)\}\Big] \end{aligned} \tag{XVI}$$

$$EE_B^A(t_i) = \mathbb{E}_t\Big[D(t,t_i)Min\{0;\Big(\Delta^- PV_A^A(t_i)+H\Big)\}1_{\{PV_A^A(t_i)>H\}}\Big] \tag{XVII}$$

2.5 *CVA and DVA: Bilateral Adjustment Formula*

The value of a derivative should normally reflect both the potential default of the counterparty to the trade and one's own potential default, with its associated gain. The risk neutral and default-risk-free valuation of the derivative would then be adjusted by both the CVA and the DVA[2].

For simplicity, we first present a bilateral CVA formula which does not assume collateral neither credit risk on collateral.

We would note $V_A^{AB}(t)$ the credit-adjusted valuation, seen from the point of view of A (subscript) and factoring in the counterparty risk and potential default of both A and B (superscript). $V_A(t)$ is still the risk neutral value of the portfolio.

$$V_A^{AB}(t) = V_A(t) + CVA_A^B(t) + DVA_A^A(t) \tag{XVIII}$$

With:

$$CVA_A^B(t) = -LGD_B\mathbb{E}_t\left[1_{\{\tau_B\leq Min(\tau_A,T)\}}D(t,\tau_B)(V_A(\tau_B))^+\right] \tag{XIX}$$

$$DVA_A^A(t) = LGD_A\mathbb{E}_t\left[1_{\{\tau_A\leq Min(\tau_B,T)\}}D(t,\tau_A)(V_A(\tau_A))^-\right] \tag{XIX}$$

We now move to a discretized time frame. We further assume that the default time on A is independent from the default time on B. Relying on the expressions obtained for CVA and DVA, we find the expressions, which would allow to introduce the effect of CSA and collateral. However, in the interest of simplicity we assume there is no credit risk on collateral.

$$CVA_A^B(t) = -LGD_B\sum_{t_i=t}^{T-1} PD_B(t_i,t_{i+1})[1-PD_A(t_i,t_{i+1})]EE_A^B(t_i) \tag{XX}$$

$$DVA_A^A(t) = -LGD_A \sum_{t_i=t}^{T-1} PD_A(t_i, t_{i+1})[1 - PD_B(t_i, t_{i+1})]NEE_A^A(t_i) \qquad \text{(XXI)}$$

The forms taken by $EE_A^B(t_i)$ and $EE_A^A(t_i)$ under a CSA with credit risk on collateral would then be the expressions previously found in the CVA and DVA formula derivations.

The bilateral CVA (BCVA) formula incorporates the two aspects.

$$BCVA_A^B(t) = CVA_A^B(t) + DVA_A^A(t) \qquad \text{(XXII)}$$

3 CVA and DVA in Finance Theory

This paragraph outlines the formal expressions for CVA and DVA as they are generally outlined in the theory of finance[3].

We first set out the framework defining a financial market with a term structure of interest rates as is generally used in financial theory, and notably in the Heath–Jarrow–Morton (HJM) model[4]. This will set the key concepts and results for pricing bonds and their associated derivatives. We then proceed with the introduction of defaultable bonds. We present the main results pertaining to the definition and calculation of the key concepts in derivatives' counterparty credit risk: CVA (Credit Valuation Adjustment) and DVA (Debt Valuation Adjustment).

We refer this paragraph in the chapters dealing with CVA and DVA mainly as being the conceptual foundation of the main concepts that are developed in a more practical perspective.

3.1 A Canonic Financial Market Framework

A continuous time trading financial market is defined in the probability space $\left(\Omega, \left\{F_{t\in[0,T_F]}\right\}, F_{T_F}, \mathbb{P}_I\right)$, with $\{F_t\}$ a filtration, viz. a series of σ-algebras such that $F_{t-1} \subset F_t$, including all measurable events and representing the information available at time t, including information on default. The market allows participants to trade in continuous time securities, including bonds and zero-coupon bonds available for a continuum of maturities over $[0, T_F]$.

$W_t = (W_{1t}, W_{2,t}, \ldots, W_{N,t})$ is a N-dimensional Brownian motion, representing the sources of uncertainty in the market, and r_t is the instantaneous or spot rate.

The value of a continuous time investment at the instantaneous spot rate r_s at time t is $B_t = e^{\int_0^t r_s ds}$, and the corresponding discount factor between t and T is $D(t,T) = \frac{B_t}{B_T} = e^{-\int_t^T r_s ds}$.

$P(t,T)$ is the price at t of the zero coupon bond providing one unit of currency at T. It is assumed that the price of a zero coupon bond follows a diffusion process defined as:

$$dP(t,T) = P(t,T)r_t dt + P(t,T)\Omega_{t,T} dW_t \tag{1}$$

and $\Omega_{t,T}$ is the instantaneous volatility matrix.

It is assumed that the financial market *offers no arbitrage opportunity* (or otherwise said does not allow any risk free gain so that it is impossible to conduct a transaction or a series of transaction involving no cost and leading to a gain under all possible states of the financial market.

It is further assumed that the financial market is *complete*. The payout of any contingent claim, defined as a measurable random variable, can be replicated by a trading strategy using initial market securities, which does not require cash after $t = 0$(the trading strategy is self-financed).

Under these assumptions, there exists a risk neutral probability, equivalent to the initial market probability $\mathbb{P}_I$, under which all assets in the market will have an instantaneous rate of return equal to the risk-free rate r_t, and such that the price at time t of any contingent claim with a payoff X_T at time T will be obtained as the expectation of X_T discounted at time t under the new risk neutral probability noted $\mathbb{P}$.

$$\mathbb{E}\left(X_T e^{-\int_t^T r_s ds} | F_t \right) \tag{2}$$

From this result, known as the fundamental pricing theorem, we obtain the price of the zero coupon $P(t,T)$:

$$P(t,T) = \mathbb{E}\left[\left(e^{-\int_t^T r_s ds} | F_t \right)\right] = \mathbb{E}_t\left[e^{-\int_t^T r_s ds} \right] = \mathbb{E}_t[D(t,T)] \tag{3}$$

Let the *continuously compounded zero-coupon rate* at t for the maturity T be Z_t^T, and let the *simply compounded rate* for the maturity T at t be $L(t,T)$. Notice that while the notation evokes the Libor rate, the simply compounded rate L_t^T does not have to be the Libor rate. Also notice that the notation $(T - t)$ is used to designate the number of business days that are applicable to the contracts and reflect the conventions for day count.

$$P(t,T) = e^{-Z_t^T(T-t)} = \frac{1}{1 + (T-t)L(t,T)} \tag{4}$$

3.2 3.2. Forward Rate Agreement (FRA) and Swap Pricing

We define a forward rate agreement (FRA) contract as a contract which pays its holder the difference in the simply compounded interest computed on a notional N at the rate $K_0 - L(T,S)$ between the two future dates T and S with $S > T$. The payout of the $FRA_{T,S}$ or its value at time S is:

$$FRA_{T,S}(S) = N[K_0 - L(T,S)](S-T) \tag{5}$$

We first assume in what follows that there is no default risk in the FRA contract: Either because the FRA contract is perfectly collateralized or guaranteed, we assume that the potential default of the counterparty to the FRA contract will not change the payout. Using (2) and (4) and taking the value at time t of the FRA one finds:

$$FRA_{T,S}(t) = N(S-T)P(t,S)\left[K_0 - \frac{1}{(S-T)}\left(\frac{P(t,T)}{P(t,S)} - 1\right)\right] \tag{6}$$

If we note $L_t^*(T,S)$ the forward value at time t of the simply compounded rate $L(T,S)$ between T and S. Designating by $P_t^*(T,S)$ the forward value at $t < T < S$ of the zero-coupon bond at T with maturity S, one has the following relation among simply compounding rates and their forward values.

$$\begin{aligned} \frac{1}{P(t,T)}\frac{1}{P_t^*(T,S)} = \frac{1}{P(t,S)} &= 1 + (S-t)L(t,S) \\ &= [1 + (T-t)L(t,T)][1 + (S-T)L_t^*(T,S)] \end{aligned} \tag{7}$$

From where one sees that the price of the $FRA_{T,S}$ at time t can be obtained simply by replacing $L(T,S)$ by its forward value at time t $L_t^*(T,S)$.

In particular, the value at the initial time t_0 of the $FRA_{T,S}$ between will be 0 (the fair price at inception for a derivative contract requiring no initial payment) if K_0, the contractual simply compounded rate in the FRA is equal to $L^*_{t_0}(T,S)$, the forward value at t_0 of the simply compounded rate

Knowing that the $FRA_{T,S}$ price at t is obtained by replacing $L(T,S)$ by its forward value $L^*_t(T,S)]$ in the payout formula, one can also apply Eq. (2), the fundamental pricing theorem, to the random payout at time S of the $FRA_{T,S}$ and find, therefore, that:

$$L^*_t(T,S) = \mathbb{E}(L(T,S)|F_t) = \mathbb{E}_t(L(T,S)) \tag{8}$$

The forward value at t of the simply compounded rate $L(T,S)$ is the expectation of $L(T,S)$ conditional on the information available at t under the risk neutral probability $\mathbb{P}$. Note again that, so far, we have assumed the $FRA_{T,S}$ contract is protected from default.

A swap is a contract with a given nominal value N, and a maturity T, in which two counterparties will exchange interest payments at as series of predefined dates $T_1, T_2, \ldots, T_n$ with $T_n = T$, with one counterparty paying based on a fixed interest rate K_0 and the other counterparty paying based on the future realized values of the floating rate. The swap can be thought of as a series of $FRA_{T_i,T_{i+1}}$ with identical contract rate K_0, or as a contract in which the holder of a fixed rate bond (the fixed leg of the swap) "swaps" their fixed coupon with the variable coupon of a floating rate note (the floating leg of the swap). A receiver swap will commit its holder to make or receive at each date $T_{i+1} (i = 0, \ldots n-1)$ the payment

$$N(T_{i+1} - T_i)[K_0 - L(T_i, T_{i+1})] \tag{9}$$

From the pricing formula for the FRA, we infer the value of a (receiver) swap simply by replacing the values of the future values of $L(T_i, T_{i+1})$ by their forward values taken at the date of pricing. This gives at time T_0.

$$V(T_0) = \sum_{i=1}^{n} P(T_0, T_i) N(T_i - T_{i-1})[K_0 - L^*_{T_0}(T_{i-1}, T_i)] \tag{10}$$

And at any later time $t < T$, the value of the swap will be given by, assuming further that $T_{h-1} < t < T_h$

$$V(t) = \sum_{i=h}^{n} P(t, T_i) N(T_i - T_{i-1})[K_0 - L^*_t(T_{i-1}, T_i)] \tag{11}$$

This pricing could have been obtained directly by applying the fundamental pricing theorem expressed in formula (2) to the series of future random cash flows of the swap

$$V(t) = \mathbb{E}_t\{\sum_{i=h}^{n} D(t,T_i)N(T_i - T_{i-1})\left[K_0 - L_t(T_{i-1},T_i)\right]\} \tag{12}$$

Noting that in the sum the factors $D(t,T_i)$ taken at t are deterministic and equal to $P(t,T_i)$. Noting $C(t,T)$ the discounted cash flows in the swap between t and T, we have:

$$V(t) = \mathbb{E}_t[C(t,T)] \tag{13}$$

This general formula would apply to any derivative generating the cash flows $C(t,T)$.

In the case of a swap which normally starts with a value of zero at the initial time T_0 (thus implying no upfront payment from either counterparty), K_0 has to be equal to a weighted average of the forward values of the variable simply compounded rate $L^*_{T_0}(T_{i-1},T_i)$. This value of K_0 is the value S_{T_0} of the fixed rate swap with maturity $T_n = T$ taken at time T_0.

$$S_{T_0} = \sum_{i=1}^{n} \frac{(T_i - T_{i-1})P(T_0,T_i)}{\sum_{i=1}^{n}(T_i - T_{i-1})P(T_0,T_i)} L^*_{T_0}(T_{i-1},T_i) \tag{14}$$

Using the relation between the forward value $L^*_{T_0}(T_{i-1},T_i)$ and the forward value of the zero-coupon bond, and noting that $\frac{1}{P(T_0,T_{i-1})}\frac{1}{P^*_{T_0}(T_{i-1},T_i)} = \frac{1}{P(T_0,T_i)}$ the swap rate can be expressed in a simpler way as shown below:

$$S_{T_0} = \frac{1 - P(T_0,T_n)}{\sum_{i=1}^{n}(T_i - T_{i-1})P(T_0,T_i)} \tag{15}$$

Assuming default risk has been fully mitigated, the swap rate at time T_0 can be considered as the rate R_{T_0} of a coupon bond, a bullet bond with principal repaid at the maturity T, issued at par at T_0 and whose cash flows would be discounted with the zero-coupon bonds $P(T_0,T_i)$. For such a bond issued at par the following relation would apply.

$$1 = \sum_{i=1}^{n} R_{T_0}(T_i - T_{i-1})P\left(T_0,T_i\right) + P\left(T_0,T_n\right) \tag{16}$$

From (13), we obtain an expression for R_{T_0} similar to that of the swap rate S_{T_0} given above in (12).

$$R_{T_0} = \frac{1 - P(T_0, T_n)}{\sum_{i=1}^{n}(T_i - T_{i-1})P(T_0, T_i)} \tag{17}$$

3.3 Defaultable Bonds Modeling

In this section, we present notations and methods generally used for defaultable instruments such as Defaultable Bonds and Credit Default Swaps. We stay focused on reduced-form models.

3.3.1 Modeling Default in a Reduced Form

In a "reduced-form" credit risk model, default is treated as an exogenous event. For any entity X, which is assumed to be exposed to the risk of default (i.e., not being able to honor its commitments to pay after the time default has been declared), the focus is on the date of default τ_X and on the probability of default. More specifically, reduced-form default risk modeling starts with the following assumption.

Knowing that (or conditional on the fact that) the entity X has not experienced a default (or has "survived") until, the probability that default can happen between t and $t + dt$ is:

$$\mathbb{P}((\tau_X \leq t + dt | \tau > t) = \lambda(t)dt \tag{18}$$

which leads to

$$\mathbb{P}_t(\tau_X > T) = \mathbb{P}(\tau_X > T | \tau_X > t) = e^{-\int_t^T \lambda(s)ds} \tag{19}$$

With τ_X the time of default of entity X and $\lambda()$ a deterministic function, called the intensity function, which characterizes the likelihood with which a default event can occur over a short time span.

In particular, at the initial time:

$$\mathbb{P}(\tau_X > t) = e^{-\int_0^t \lambda(s)ds} \tag{20}$$

3.3.2 Pricing of Defaultable Bonds

Let us consider a zero-coupon defaultable bond issued by entity X characterized by the first time of default τ_X and the intensity of default λ_X. The price, taken at time t, of the defaultable zero-coupon bond with maturity T issued by entity X is noted $P_X(t, T)$. The corresponding rate of this defaultable zero-coupon bond is noted $Z_{X,t}^{T} = Z_{t}^{T} + s_{X,t}^{T}$, with $s_{X,t}^{T}$ the credit spread of the entity X relative to the default-free zero coupon. We also assume, in order to simplify notations, that, even if default happens before T, it is only at T that the payment of a unit of currency will not be honored by the defaulting entity. We finally assume that, in case of default, the payment of the due unit of currency is replaced instead of the payment of R_X units (with $R_X < 1$), which is equivalent to set the LGD_X, the Loss Given Default ($LGD_X = 1 - R_X$)to be different from zero, as it would be in a non-default setting.

The price $P_X(t, T)$ will be expressed as the average or the expectation, under the risk neutral probability, of the values taken by the zero-coupon bond over the two set of events, those whether the default has happened and those where it has not. For this purpose, we will use the event indicator function 1_A which takes the value 1 if the event A has occurred or 0 otherwise. At time T, if default has occurred $1_{\{\tau_X \leq T\}} = 1$ and the payout on the zero-coupon bond is not 1 but R. If default has not occurred $1_{\{\tau_X \leq T\}} = 1$, the zero-coupon pays one unit of currency. Also bear in mind that F_t represents all the information available at t including information on default; therefore the events $\{\tau_X \leq T\}$ and $\{\tau_X > T\}$ are included in F_t; furthermore, the events $\{\tau_X \leq t\}$ and $\{\tau_X > t\}$ have been realized at t.

$$P_X(t, T) = \mathbb{E}\{R1_{\{\tau_X \leq T\}} + 1_{\{\tau_X > T\}}|F_t\} = \mathbb{E}_t\left[D(t, T)[R1_{\{\tau_X \leq T\}} + 1_{\{\tau_X > T\}}]\right] \quad (21)$$

This gives the following expression:

$$P_X(t, T) = P(t, T)[R\mathbb{P}_t(\tau_X \leq T) + \mathbb{P}_t(\tau_X > T) \quad (22)$$

$$P_X(t, T) = P(t, T)[(1 - R)\mathbb{P}_t(\tau_X > T) + R] = P(t, T)[\mathbb{P}_t(\tau_X > T)LGD + (1 - LGD)] \quad (23)$$

$$P_X(t, T) = \mathbb{E}_t\left[e^{-\int_t^T r_s ds}\right]\mathbb{E}_t\left[e^{-\int_t^T \lambda_X(s)ds}LGD + (1 - LGD)\right] \quad (24)$$

If we note $r_{X,t}$ the instantaneous spot rate for entity X and if we assume LGD is equal to 1 (that is there is no recovery in case of default), we obtain the following intuitive expressions:

$$\begin{aligned} P_X(t, T) &= \mathbb{E}_t\left[e^{-\int_t^T r_{X,s} ds}\right] = \mathbb{E}_t\left[e^{-\int_t^T r_s ds}\right]\mathbb{E}_t\left[e^{-\int_t^T \lambda_X(s)ds}\right] \\ &= \mathbb{E}_t\left[e^{-\int_t^T (r_s + \lambda_X(s))ds}\right] \end{aligned} \quad (25)$$

In this case, the default intensity function for entity X is equal to its instantaneous credit spread.

$$r_{X,t} = r_t + \lambda_X(t) \tag{26}$$

Using now the defaultable zero-coupon rates and spreads and defining $\Lambda_{X,t}^T$ as the continuously compounded default intensity by: $\mathbb{E}_t\left[e^{-\Lambda_{X,t}^T(T-t)}\right] = \mathbb{E}_t\left[e^{-\int_t^T \lambda_X(s)ds}\right]$

We also obtain:

$$Z_{X,t}^T = Z_t^T + \Lambda_{X,t}^T \tag{27}$$

Now, if we no longer assume LGD to be equal to 1 and rewrite the expression (21) using $Z_{X,t}^T$, Z_t^T and $\Lambda_{X,t}^T$, we can derive a first-order linear approximation for the defaultable zero-coupon rate:

$$e^{-Z_{X,t}^T(T-t)} = e^{-Z_t^T(T-t)}\left\{LGDe^{-\Lambda_{X,t}^T(T-t)} + (1 - LGD)\right\} \tag{28}$$

$$Z_{X,t}^T \cong Z_t^T + \Lambda_{X,t}^T LGD \tag{29}$$

We then see that the credit spread of X can be approximated by the product of its default intensity and its Loss Given Default.

3.4 *Defaultable Swaps Modeling: CVA*

The methods for modeling defaultable bonds were established in the 1990s, taking the point of view of an investor located, so to speak, "outside" of the market, meaning that there was point in including the credit quality of the investor itself in the model.

When the attention turned to derivatives and swaps from the early 2000s, the bilateral nature of the swap and of the majority of derivatives contracts had to be factored in. What we mean by bilateral nature is that the default risk of both counterparties to the swap contract is an intrinsic part of the contract as it directly influences all future payouts in the swap an therefore influences its price.

As already seen above (see paragraphs above covering formulae (5) to (15)), a swap between two entities A and B would normally start with a value of 0. Then, over its life, the price or the MtM, the Mark-to-Market, may become positive or negative. Seen from A, a positive MtM means that the net present value of the payments between A and B is positive for A and negative for B. A is therefore faced with counterparty credit risk, the default risk of B. To mitigate this risk, A would typically require B to post-collateral, to deliver in cash or in securities an amount equal to the MtM. But the MtM of the swap may change sign over time, B may in turn see a positive MtM from its standpoint while A has a negative MtM. This time it would be the turn of counterparty B to be exposed to the default risk of A and to require collateral.

A counterparty A with a positive MtM should include in the price of the swap the effect of default. This adjustment is called the Credit Value Adjustment.

At the same time, the fact that counterparty A may also default, and therefore may not honor all payments due to counterparty B, should also be reflected in the price. This adjustment is called the Debt Value Adjustment.

3.4.1 CVA: Formal Expression Without Collateral

Considering the swap and derivative valuation formulae (11) to (13) given above, which implicitly assumed no default, we make the two counterparties to the contract explicit and, referring to them as A and B, we value the derivative from the point of view of A assuming, as a first step, that B can default while A is assumed to remain immune to default.

We call $V_A(t)$ the value of the swap or the derivative seen from A in the absence of default risk on B and $V_A^B(t)$ the same value once taken into account the default risk of B. We call τ_B the time at which B would default. This means that the event $\{\tau_B > T\}$ is the event: "no default from B over the life of the contract" while the complementary event $\{\tau_B \leq T\}$ depicts a default from B. Using formula (13) above, and designating by $C_A(t, T)]$ the discounted value of all cash flows in the swap, seen from A, in the absence of any default risk, we write the value of the derivative in the absence of default risk as:

$$V_A(t) = \mathbb{E}_t[C_A(t, T)] \tag{30}$$

If we introduce the default on B we can split the expectation into two parts that correspond to the events $\{\tau_B > T\}$ and $\{\tau_B \leq T\}$, using the event indicator functions: $1_{\{\tau_B > T\}}$, which returns the value 1 if B does not default and 0 otherwise, and $1_{\{\tau_B \leq T\}}$ which indicates 1 if B defaults and 0 otherwise.

If there is no default by B, i.e., we are within the $\{\tau_B > T\}$ event, the same cash flows as in the default-risk-free situation prevail.

Therefore, among the two parts of the expectation, the part referenced by $1_{\{\tau_B>T\}}$ will simply be: $\mathbb{E}_t\left[1_{\{\tau_B>T\}}C_A(t,T)\right]$.

Looking now at the event of default $\{\tau_B \leq T\}$, we need to apply the expectation operator to all the possible cash flows of the derivative.

Before the time of default τ_B, all cash flows hold and their discounted value at t is simply equal to $C_A(t,\tau_B)$.

Once default by B has occurred, there are two cases:

- If the derivative value is positive to A at time τ_B: $V_A(\tau_B) > 0$ or $(V_A(\tau_B))^+ = Max(V_A(\tau_B), 0) > 0$, then A will be paid the recovery value at τ_B, which is $R_B(V_A(\tau_B))^+$;
- If the derivative value is negative to A: $V_A(\tau_B) < 0$ or $(-V_A(\tau_B))^+ > 0$, then A will have to pay the value of the contract to B since the contract terminates at its Mark-to-Market at the time of default.

This leads to the formula:

$$\begin{aligned} V_A^B(t) =& \mathbb{E}_t\left[1_{\{\tau_B>T\}}C_A(t,T)\right] \\ &+ \mathbb{E}_t\left[1_{\{\tau_B\leq T\}}[C_A(t,\tau_B) + D(t,\tau_B)\{R_B(V_A(\tau_B))^+ - (-V_A(\tau_B))^+\}]\right] \end{aligned} \tag{31}$$

The derivative pricing formula can be expressed in a more intuitive way.

Having in mind that $C_A(t,T)$ represents the discounted value at t of the derivative's cash flows in the absence of default, one can write, in the situation of default (with $1_{\{\tau_B\leq T\}} = 1$):

$$1_{\{\tau_B\leq T\}}C_A(t,T) = 1_{\{\tau_B\leq T\}}[C_A(t,\tau_B) + D(t,\tau_B)\{R_B(V_A(\tau_B))^+ - (-V_A(\tau_B))^+\}] \tag{32}$$

If we write $1_{\{\tau_B\leq T\}}C_A(t,\tau_B)$ as a function of $1_{\{\tau_B\leq T\}}C_A(t,T)$ using (32) and given that:

$$\mathbb{E}_t[1_{\{\tau_B\leq T\}}C_A(t,T) + 1_{\{\tau_B>T\}}C_A(t,T)] = \mathbb{E}_t[C_A(t,T)] = V_A(t) \tag{33}$$

We obtain:

$$V_A^B(t) = \underbrace{\mathbb{E}_t[C_A(t,T)]}_{\substack{\text{Risk neutral} \\ \text{Default risk} \\ \text{Free value}}} - \underbrace{\mathbb{E}_t\left[\mathbb{1}_{\{\tau_B\leq T\}}D(t,\tau_B)(1-R_B)\left(V_A(\tau_B)\right)^+\right]}_{\text{CVA: expected loss due to the default of B}} \tag{34}$$

The expression of $V_A^B(t)$ is easily interpreted as the value of the derivative in the absence of default risk minus the expectation of the loss due to a default of counterparty B. The second part is the CVA, the credit value adjustment on counterparty B, seen from A. So, ignoring for the moment A's own default risk we have the derivative valuation expression:

$$V_A^B(t) = V_A(t) + CVA_A^B(t) \tag{35}$$

Keeping the same methodology and using the event indicator functions, we now introduce the possibility that A may also be in default. In an event of default A may have to pay less to B than would have been required in a non-default world.

3.4.2 CVA: Formula in a Discretized Time Frame Without Collateral

We now transform the formal expression of the CVA in (34) in a discretized framework which is going to lead to the expressions discussed in paragraph 1. In doing so, we establish the link between theory and actual implementation of CVA calculations: practical methods for financial reporting and development of CVA computation systems.

We assume that time is discretized over the life of the portfolio with a series of time points: $t_i i = 0 \ldots N$.

The CVA expression in (34) is:

$$-\mathbb{E}_t\left[1_{\{\tau_B \leq T\}} D(t, \tau_B)(1 - R_B)(V_A(\tau_B))^+\right] \tag{36}$$

and can be rewritten in a discretized form as:

$$-\sum_{t_i=t}^{T-1} \mathbb{E}_t[1_{\{t_i \leq \tau_B < t_{i+1}\}} D(t, t_i)(1 - R_B)(V_A(t_i))^+] \tag{37}$$

Given that the recovery rate is not random and assuming that probabilities of default are independent of the change in value of the derivative portfolio (37) gives:

$$-\sum_{t_i=t}^{T}(1 - R_B)\mathbb{E}_t[1_{\{t_i \leq \tau_B < t_{i+1}\}}]\mathbb{E}_t[D(t, t_i)(V_A(t_i))^+] \tag{38}$$

We note $EE_A^B(t_i)$ the expected discounted positive value of the portfolio at t_i from the point of view of A.

At the same time, we note that the probability of default of B between the times t_i and t_{i+1} is simply:

$$PD_B(t_i, t_{i+1}) = \mathbb{E}_t[1_{\{t_i \leq \tau_B < t_{i+1}\}}] \tag{39}$$

Therefore, the expression (38) giving the CVA can be rewritten, in a discretized form, as:

$$CVA_A^B(t) = -(1 - R_B) \sum_{t_i=t}^{T-1} PD_B(t_i, t_{i+1}) EE_A^B(t_i) \tag{40}$$

This is the expression presented in paragraph 1 above.

In (40), we can relate the probability of default to the credit spread of counterparty B.

$$PD_B(t_i, t_{i+1}) = \mathbb{P}(\tau_B \geq t_i | \tau_B \geq t) - \mathbb{P}(\tau_B \geq t_{i+1} | \tau_B \geq t) \tag{41}$$

But we know that $\mathbb{P}(\tau_B \geq t_i | \tau_B \geq t) = e^{-\Lambda_{B,t}^{t_i}(t_i - t)}$

With $\Lambda_{B,t}^{t_i}$ the continuously compounded default intensity for B at the horizon t_i taken at time t.

We also showed in formula (29) (shown for zero coupon defaultable bond) that the continuously compounded default intensity for maturity t_i could be approximated as:

$$\Lambda_{B,t}^{t_i} \approx \frac{s_{B,t}^{t_i}}{LGD_B} \text{ with } s_{B,t}^{t_i} \text{ the credit spread of B at the maturity } t_i \text{ taken at time } t. \tag{42}$$

$$PD_B(t_i, t_{i+1}) = \mathbb{P}(\tau_B \geq t_i | \tau_B \geq t) - \mathbb{P}(\tau_B \geq t_{i+1} | \tau_B \geq t) \tag{43}$$

$$PD_B(t_i, t_{i+1}) = e^{-\Lambda_{B,t}^{t_i}(t_i - t)} - e^{-\Lambda_{B,t}^{t_{i+1}}(t_{i+1} - t)} \tag{44}$$

$$PD_B(t_i, t_{i+1}) = e^{-\frac{s_{B,t}^{t_i}}{LGD_B}(t_i - t)} - e^{-\frac{s_{B,t}^{t_{i+1}}}{LGD_B}(t_{i+1} - t)} \tag{45}$$

We obtain therefore the alternative formulation for the CVA:

$$CVA_A^B(t) = -LGD_B \sum_{t_i=t}^{T-1} [e^{-\frac{s_{B,t}^{t_i}}{LGD_B}(t_i - t)} - e^{-\frac{s_{B,t}^{t_{i+1}}}{LGD_B}(t_{i+1} - t)}] EE_A^B(t_i) \tag{46}$$

Let us note that, if we were to assume spreads are small and $e^{-\frac{s_{B,t}^{t_i}}{LGD_B}(t_i-t)} \cong 1 - \frac{s_{B,t}^{t_i}}{LGD_B}(t_i - t)$; if we also assume the spread of B is constant and, finally, as a very drastic simplification, that the Expected Exposure is constant over time, and equal to its average over time, the discounted Expected Positive Exposure (EPE), we would obtain the simple, intuitive formula:

$$CVA_A^B(t) \cong -s_{B,t}^T EPE_A^B(t) \tag{47}$$

The CVA is homogeneous to the discounted expected positive exposure on the counterparty B times its credit spread.

3.4.3 CVA: Formal Expression with Collateral

The CSA in an ISDA governs the posting of collateral for an entire derivatives portfolio—or *Netting Set.* Let us first introduce notations to reflect the fact that we now consider a portfolio (or Netting Set) of N derivatives indexed by $k = 1..N$.

The credit risk adjusted of every derivative at time t is noted:

$$V_{A,k}^B(t) \tag{48}$$

And the value of the portfolio will be noted PV (for portfolio value).

$$PV_A^B(t) = \sum_{k=1}^{N} V_{A,k}^B(t) \tag{49}$$

We assume the credit risk of the portfolio is mitigated with collateral. We call H the value of the *Threshold* (we assume the *Minimum Transfer Amount* is 0).

We note the *Replacement Period* Δt, and we note $\Delta^+ V_{A,k}^B(t)$ the positive variation (increase) of the value of a derivative over the Replacement Period taken at time t.

For any derivative in the portfolio, taken separately, the expected exposure, conditional to the default taking place at time t_i, is broken down into two components by the presence of collateral, depending on whether the value of the portfolio is above or below Threshold.

If the value of the portfolio stands above Threshold, that is if $PV_A^B(t_i) \geq H$, the exposure caused by this specific derivative k is equal to:

$$H\frac{V^B_{A,k}(t_i)}{PV^B_A(t_i)} + \Delta^+ V^B_{A,k}(t_i) \tag{50}$$

If the value of the portfolio is below the Threshold at the time of default, the exposure caused by the specific derivative is simply the value of this derivative at time t_i since it is not protected by collateral, plus, again the increase in the MtM over the Replacement Period.

$$V^B_{A,k}(t_i) + \Delta^+ V^B_{A,k}(t_i) \tag{51}$$

In (50), the first term is the attribution to the derivative k of a fraction of the Threshold (since the Threshold is lost) equal to its pro-rata in the whole value of the portfolio. Also note that this value could be separately negative. But we will add all the exposures in the Netting Set to go to the end of the calculation; some of the derivatives may have a negative contribution to the exposure, which is what one would expect in a Netting Set of derivatives which are not all identical and may react differently to changes in market variables.

In (50), the second term is simply the change in value of derivative k over the Replacement Period, which is going to enter into the expectation.

Taken at time t, the Expected Exposure of derivative k should B default in the interval $[t_i, t_{i+1}]$ writes:

$$\begin{aligned}
&EE^B_{A,k}(t_i) = \\
&\quad \mathbb{E}_t\left[1_{\left\{0 \le PV^B_{A,k}(t_i) \le H\right\}} D(t,t_i)[V^B_{A,k}(t_i) + \frac{\Delta^+ V^B_{A,k}(t_i)}{LGD_B}]\right] \quad \text{(if below Threshold0} \\
&\quad + \mathbb{E}_t\left[1_{\left\{H < PV^B_{A,k}(t_i)\right\}} D(t,t_i+\Delta t)\frac{\Delta^+ V^B_{A,k}(t_i)}{LGD_B}\right] \\
&\qquad\qquad \text{(above Threshold : } \Delta^+ V^B_{A,k}(t_i)) \\
&\quad + \mathbb{E}_t\left[1_{\left\{H < PV^B_{A,k}(t_i)\right\}} D(t,t_i+\Delta t) H \frac{\Delta^+ V^B_{A,k}(t_i)}{PV^B_A(t_i)}\right] \\
&\qquad\qquad \text{(above Threshold, pro} - \text{rata of lost Threshold)}
\end{aligned} \tag{52}$$

To complete the CVA calculation, we only have to weigh this Expected Exposure in the interval $[t_i, t_{i+1}]$ by the probability that default takes place in this interval, which is $PD_B(t_i, t_{i+1})$, and then sum over the date points t_i, and over all the N derivatives in the portfolio.

$$CVA_A^B(t) = \sum_{k=1}^{N} CVA_{A,k}^B(t) \tag{53}$$

With:

$$CVA_{A,k}^B(t) = -LGD_B \sum_{t_i=t}^{T} PD_B(t_i, t_{i+1}) EE_{A,k}^B(t_i) \tag{54}$$

Therefore:

$$CVA_A^B(t) = -LGD_B \sum_{k=1}^{N} \sum_{t_i=t}^{T} PD_B(t_i, t_{i+1}) EE_{A,k}^B(t_i) \tag{55}$$

If we develop the Expected Exposure, we can obtain an expression which remains relatively simple when we aggregate at portfolio's level (summing the *ks*).

To further simplify, we will assume that $D(t, t_i + \Delta t) \cong D(t, t_i)$. With this, we obtain the expression:

$$CVA_A^B(t) = -LGD_B \sum_{t_i=t}^{T} PD_B(t_i, t_{i+1}) EE_A^B(t_i) \tag{56}$$

$$\begin{aligned} EE_A^B(t_i) = \mathbb{E}_t \Bigg[& D(t, t_i) \{ 1_{\{0 \leq PV_A^B(t_i) \leq H\}} (PV_A^B(t_i) \\ & + \frac{\Delta^+ PV_A^B(t_i)}{LGD_B}) + 1_{\{H < PV_A^B(t_i)\}} \left(H + \frac{\Delta^+ PV_A^B(t_i)}{LGD_B} \right) \} \Bigg] \end{aligned} \tag{57}$$

$$CVA_A^B(t) =$$

$$-LGD_B \sum_{t_i=t}^{T} PD_B(t_i, t_{i+1}) \mathbb{E}_t \left[D(t, t_i) \{ \underbrace{\mathbb{1}_{\{0 \leq PV_A^B(t_i) \leq H\}} (PV_A^B(t_i) + \frac{\Delta^+ PV_A^B(t_i)}{LGD_B})}_{} + \underbrace{\mathbb{1}_{\{H < PV_A^B(t_i)\}} \left(H + \frac{\Delta^+ PV_A^B(t_i)}{LGD_B} \right)}_{} \} \right]$$

For Basel's "non-covered entities"

Exposure below Threshold Positive Mark to Market + increase in portfolio price over replacement period

Exposure above Threshold Threshold + increase in Portfolio price over replacement period

(58)

In the chapter on collateral, we learned about one of the main flows of collateral: the fact that posted collateral (in variation margins) was subject to default risk.

We also learned that, among dealer banks and systematically important non-financial entities, posting an Initial Margin, designed to be larger than the maximum (99% level) potential MtM increase over the Replacement Period, was recommended by the Basel Committee to be made mandatory among regulators. This is becoming reality in the USA from September 2016.

If we want a practical CVA formula that really prices counterparty risk, how should we reflect these aspects in the formula?

The first comment is that formula (56) applies only in the absence of Initial Margin. For bank dealers and systemically important market participants, with mandatory Initial Margin equal to the 99% PFE over the replacement period, we can reasonably assume that the term ΔPV_A^B is no longer a risk.

So, for Basel-covered entities: financial firms and systematically important non-financial firms, the CVA in expression (56) should read:

$$CVA_A^B(t) = -LGD_B \sum_{t_i=t}^{T} PD_B(t_i, t_{i+1})\, \mathbb{E}_t \Big[D(t,t_i) \{ \underbrace{\mathbb{1}_{\{0 \le PV_A^B(t_i) \le H\}} PV_A^B(t_i)}_{\text{Exposure below Threshold Positive Mark to Market of Portfolio}} + \underbrace{\mathbb{1}_{\{H < PV_A^B(t_i)\}} H}_{\text{Exposure = Threshold}} \} \Big] \tag{59}$$

For Financial Firms & systematically important Non-Financial Firms with Initial Margin

For all other entities, formula (56) remains valid.

Let us now deal with the credit risk on posted collateral.

3.4.4 CVA: Formal Expression with Credit Risk on Collateral

In the chapter on collateral, we learned that international banking regulation decided to eliminate the risk of default on collateral only for the Initial Margin. For collateral posted as variation margin, posted collateral is exposed to the risk of default of the receiving entity. More precisely, since this variation margin matches a negative MtM, the exposure on the posted collateral is covered by the negative MtM it represents: If collateral is lost, the negative MtM exposure also extinguishes and the surviving firm would not pay the negative MtM unless it receives its collateral back. However, this is no longer valid if there is an increase in MtM during the replacement period, an increase such that it would no longer match the posted collateral. We also note to take account the fact that collateral is only posted above Threshold: Since things are seen from A's point of view, A posts collateral only when the MtM of the Netting Set is negative and below—H (the value of the Threshold with a negative sign). Finally, we need to take into account the fact that A has posted the MtM of the portfolio at the time of default less the threshold.

This leads to an expected value of the loss on posted collateral equal to:

$$LGD_B \sum_{t_i=t}^{T} PD_B(t_i, t_{i+1}) \mathbb{E}_t \left[D(t, t_i) 1_{\{PV_A^B(t_i) \leq -H\}} \{\Delta^+ PV_A^B(t_i) - H\} \right] \quad (60)$$

If we integrate this aspect into the value of the CVA, we would have the expression below with the new term: $-NEE_A^B(t_i)$, which is identical for all entities either covered by the new Basel margining regulation or not (the regulation does not address the risk on variation margin). However, we still have two expressions for the term $EE_A^B(t_i)$

$$CVA_A^B(t) = -LGD_B \sum_{t_i=t}^{T} PD_B(t_i, t_{i+1}) \left[EE_A^B(t_i) - NEE_A^B(t_i) \right] \quad (61)$$

With:

- the discounted Expected Exposure term $EE_A^B(t_i)$ similar to the previous formula without default risk on collateral, with two versions, one for Basel-covered entities and one for non-covered entities;
- the additional discounted Negative Expected Exposure term $NEE_A^B(t_i)$, reflecting the risk on posted collateral

$$EE_A^B(t_i) = \mathbb{E}_t \left[D(t, t_i) \{ 1_{\{0 \leq PV_A^B(t_i) \leq H\}} PV_A^B(t_i) + 1_{\{H < PV_A^B(t_i)\}} H \} \right] \quad \text{For Basel} - \text{covered entities} \quad (62)$$

And for non-covered entities

$$EE_A^B(t_i) = \mathbb{E}_t \left[D(t, t_i) \{ 1_{\{0 \leq PV_A^B(t_i) \leq H\}} (PV_A^B(t_i) + \frac{\Delta^+ PV_A^B(t_i)}{LGD_B}) + 1_{\{H < PV_A^B(t_i)\}} \left(H + \frac{\Delta^+ PV_A^B(t_i)}{LGD_B} \right) \} \right] \quad (63)$$

$$-NEE_A^B(t_i) = \mathbb{E}_t \left[D(t, t_i) \{ \Delta^+ PV_A^B(t_i) - H \} 1_{\{PV_A^B(t_i) < -H\}} \right] \quad (64)$$

3.5 DVA

3.5.1 DVA Formal Expression Without Collateral

In order to better capture the very concept of DVA, we now assume that B is a default-free counterparty while A is now subject to the risk of being in default and seeks to reflect this possibility in the pricing of the derivative of the swap between A and B.

Compared to the default-risk-free value of the derivative seen from A's point of view: $V_A(t)$, we now introduce the notation $V_A^A(t)$ to reflect the fact that the valuation is now adjusted for the possible default of A. Looking at the default risk of A alone allows us to capture the DVA as the adjustment to be made to the valuation of the derivative contract.

We follow the same line of reasoning as the one for the default risk of B. Starting from the standard default-risk-free valuation formula: $V_A(t) = \mathbb{E}_t[C_A(t,T)]$, we split the expectation according to the two complementary events $\{\tau_A > T\}$ and $\{\tau_A \leq T\}$. By the same reasoning as above, we know that:

Among the two parts of the expectation, the part referenced by $1_{\{\tau_A > T\}}$ will simply be: $\mathbb{E}_t\left[1_{\{\tau_A > T\}} C_A(t,T)\right]$.

The part referenced by $1_{\{\tau_A \leq T\}}$ will apply the expectation operator to the cash flows of the derivative knowing that A has defaulted at time τ_A.

Before the time of default τ_A, all cash flows hold and their discounted value at t is simply equal to $C_A(t, \tau_A)$.

Once defaults has occurred at τ_A, the same analysis for payments, depending on the sign of the MtM seen from A, applies as in the CVA section above.

The value of the derivative adjusted for the default risk of A, and assuming there is no default risk on B is:

$$\begin{aligned} V_A^A(t) =& \mathbb{E}_t\left[1_{\{\tau_A > T\}} C_A(t,T)\right] \\ &+ \mathbb{E}_t\left[1_{\{\tau_A \leq T\}} [C_A(t,\tau_A) + D(t,\tau_A)\{(V_A(\tau_A))^+ - R_A(-V_A(\tau_A))^+\}]\right] \end{aligned} \tag{65}$$

Notice that in the expression above, once default has occurred, the value of the derivative is unchanged if, seen from A, the MtM of the derivative is positive: $(V_A(\tau_A))^+ > 0$. But is on the other hand A had a negative value in the derivative at the time of default τ_A: $(-V_A(\tau_A))^+ > 0$, A only pays the recovery value

$$R_A(-V_A(\tau_A))^+ \tag{66}$$

As in the CVA section, we can obtain a more intuitive expression for $V_A^A(t)$, bearing in mind that, since $C_A(t, T)$ represents the discounted value at t of the derivative's cash flows in the absence of default, one can write in the situation of default (with $1_{\{\tau_A \leq T\}} = 1$):

$$1_{\{\tau_A \leq T\}} C_A(t, T) = 1_{\{\tau_A \leq T\}} [C_A(t, \tau_A) + D(t, \tau_A)\{(V_A(\tau_A))^+ - R_A(-V_A(\tau_A))^+\}] \quad (67)$$

Using again the fact that:

$$\mathbb{E}_t[1_{\{\tau_A \leq T\}} C_A(t, T) + 1_{\{\tau_A > T\}} C_A(t, T)] = \mathbb{E}_t[C_A(t, T)] = V_A(t) \quad (68)$$

And replacing $1_{\{\tau_A \leq T\}}[C_A(t, \tau_A)]$ in (67) by its expression as a function of $\mathbb{E}_t\left[1_{\{\tau_A > T\}} C_A(t, T)\right]$, we find:

$$V_A^A(t) = \underbrace{\mathbb{E}_t[C_A(t,T)]}_{\text{Default risk-free value}} + \underbrace{\mathbb{E}_t\left[\mathbb{1}_{\{\tau_A \leq T\}} D(t, \tau_A)(1 - R_A)\left(V_A(\tau_A)\right)^+\right]}_{\text{DVA: Expected gain if A defaults (discounted at t)}} \quad (69)$$

The expression of $V_A^A(t)$ can be easily interpreted as the value of the derivative in the absence of default risk plus the expectation of the gain due to A's own default. The second part is the DVA, the Debt Value Adjustment on A's own default risk seen from A. Ignoring now the default risk of B but considering the default risk of A alone, we have the derivative valuation expression with the Debt Value Adjustment:

$$V_A^A(t) = V_A(t) + DVA_A^A(t) \quad (70)$$

$$DVA_A^A(t) = LGD_A \mathbb{E}_t\left[1_{\{\tau_A \leq T\}} D(t, \tau_A)(V_A(\tau_A))^+\right] \quad (71)$$

Assuming the default time is independent from the market variables driving the exposure this becomes.

$$DVA_A^A(t) = LGD_A \mathbb{E}_t\left[1_{\{\tau_A \leq T\}}\right] \mathbb{E}_t\left[D(t, \tau_A)(V_A(\tau_A))^+\right] \quad (72)$$

Although correct from an analytical point of view, there is something paradoxical in reflecting one's own possible default in the valuation of a derivative. In particular, the expression of the derivative's valuation in (70) shows that A would realize a MtM gain if its probability of default increases.

3.5.2 DVA Formula in a Discretized Time Frame Without Collateral

As we did for the CVA, and using the same notations for the time points, we rewrite the expression of the DVA in a discretized way as below:

$$DVA_A^A(t) = \sum_{t_i=t}^{T} \mathbb{E}_t[1_{\{t_i \leq \tau_A < t_{i+1}\}} D(t,t_i)(1-R_A)(V_A(t_i))^+] \quad (73)$$

Like for the DVA, we use the fact that the recovery rate is not random and that we assumed the probabilities of default are independent of the change in value of the derivative portfolio (59) gives:

$$\sum_{t_i=t}^{T} LGD_A \mathbb{E}_t[1_{\{t_i \leq \tau_A < t_{i+1}\}}]\mathbb{E}_t[D(t,t_i)(V_A(t_i))^+] \quad (74)$$

We note $NEE_A^A(t_i)$ the expected discounted negative value of the portfolio at t_i from the point of view of A.

$$NEE_A^A(t_i) = -\mathbb{E}_t[D(t,t_i)(V_A(t_i))^+] \quad (75)$$

Since the probability of default of A between the times t_i and t_{i+1} is simply:

$$PD_A(t_i, t_{i+1}) = \mathbb{E}_t[1_{\{t_i \leq \tau_A < t_{i+1}\}}] \quad (76)$$

Then, the expression (60) giving the CVA can be rewritten, in a discretized form, as:

$$DVA_A^A(t) = -LGD_A \sum_{t_i=t}^{T} PD_A(t_i, t_{i+1}) NEE_A^A(t_i) \quad (77)$$

This expression in (75) is the one outlined in paragraph 2 above.

We can further refine (75) by expressing the probability of default of A as a function of its credit spread.

$$PD_A(t_i, t_{i+1}) = \mathbb{P}(\tau_A \geq t_i | \tau_A \geq t) - \mathbb{P}(\tau_A \geq t_{i+1} | \tau_A \geq t) \quad (78)$$

Knowing that $\mathbb{P}(\tau_A \geq t_i | \tau_A \geq t) = e^{-\Lambda_{A,t}^{t_i}(t_i - t)}$

With $\Lambda_{A,t}^{t_i}$ the continuously compounded default intensity for A at the horizon t_i taken at time t.

And knowing that the continuously compounded default intensity for maturity t_i can be approximated as:

$$\Lambda_{A,t}^{t_i} \approx \frac{s_{A,t}^{t_i}}{LGD_A} \text{ with } s_{A,t}^{t_i} \text{ the credit spread of A at the maturity } t_i \text{ taken at time } t. \quad (79)$$

$$PD_A(t_i, t_{i+1}) = \mathbb{P}(\tau_A \geq t_i | \tau_A \geq t) - \mathbb{P}(\tau_A \geq t_{i+1} | \tau_A \geq t) \tag{80}$$

$$PD_A(t_i, t_{i+1}) = e^{-\Lambda_{A,t}^{t_i}(t_i - t)} - e^{-\Lambda_{A,t}^{t_{i+1}}(t_{i+1} - t)} \tag{81}$$

$$PD_A(t_i, t_{i+1}) = e^{-\frac{s_{A,t}^{t_i}}{LGD_A}(t_i - t)} - e^{-\frac{s_{A,t}^{t_{i+1}}}{LGD_A}(t_{i+1} - t)} \tag{82}$$

We obtain the alternative formulation for the DVA:

$$DVA_A^A(t) = -LGD_A \sum_{t_i = t}^{T} [e^{-\frac{s_{A,t}^{t_i}}{LGD_A}(t_i - t)} - e^{-\frac{s_{A,t}^{t_{i+1}}}{LGD_A}(t_{i+1} - t)}] NEE_A^A(t_i) \tag{83}$$

If we make drastic approximations like in the case of the CVA, we would similarly find that the DVA would simplify to:

$$DVA_A^A(t) \cong -s_{A,t}^T NEE_A^A \tag{84}$$

The DVA is homogeneous to the spread of A times the average negative expected exposure of A.

3.5.3 DVA Formal Expression for a Portfolio with Collateral

Using the same notations as in the CVA case, we consider a Netting Set of N derivatives indexed by $k = 1..N$.

The value of every derivative adjusted with the credit risk of A is noted, at time t:

$$V_{A,k}^A(t) \tag{85}$$

And the value of the portfolio, adjusted with the default risk of A, will be noted $PV_A^A(t)$

$$PV_A^A(t) = \sum_{k=1}^{N} V_{A,k}^A(t) \tag{86}$$

We assume the presence of collateral, with H the value of the *Threshold* and without *Minimum Transfer Amount*. This time are interested in the times when the value is negative for A.

Similar to the CVA case, for any derivative in the portfolio, taken separately, the expected negative exposure, conditional to the default taking place at time t_i, can be broken down into two components in the presence of collateral, depending whether the value of the portfolio is above or below Threshold at the time of default.

The Expected Exposure in the CVA calculation, consisting in the potential increase in the MtM during the replacement period, is matched by an equivalent in the DVA calculation. As per the ISDA terms, the value of the claim for the surviving entity is equal to the average of quotes received from swap dealers over "a reasonable period of time." So the Negative Expected Exposure will include the variation in the MtM in a way similar to the CVA. There is a difference a slight however in the calculation. In the CVA calculation, the potential uncollateralized increase of the MtM is measured by a 10-day or a 20-day expected increase in MtM, in line with regulation. In the DVA, the potential increase in the Negative Expected Exposure is also the expected change over a number of days. The number of days will be subject to the legal interpretation of "a reasonable period of time" for the surviving counterparty to receive quotes.

Similar to CVA calculations in paragraph 1.3 above, the new Basel regulation on initial margining opens two cases in the DVA calculation. For "covered entities" in the March 2015 regulation, the systematically important non-financial firms and the financial firms, the additional exposure due to the increase of the MtM after default, whose maximum amount is estimated by the PFE, will be covered by the Initial Margin. The Initial Margin has the status of segregated collateral (see chapter on collateral) and the defaulting entity cannot default on it. So there is no DVA gain, due to the change in MtM shortly after default, for counterparties that are "covered entities" in the sense of this regulation. For non-covered entities however, such a DVA gain remains.

If the value of the portfolio stands above Threshold, in absolute value, that is below Threshold for a negative MtM or $PV_A^A(t_i) \leq -H$, the amount due by A in case of default at time t_i would be - $PV_A^A(t_i)$ (if we assume that the MtM $PV_A^A(t_i)$ is negative from the point of view of A, we write the amount due by A as a positive number and therefore write: $-PV_A^A(t_i)$. Of this owed amount, only -$PV_A^A(t_i) - H$ would be collateralized. Upon default, A would still owe the Threshold H but would only pay the fraction equal to the recovery rate. If we attribute to the derivative k the pro-rata value of the Threshold, the Negative Expected

Exposure at time t_i coming from derivative, we would add the pro-rata of the Threshold to the change over the reasonable of time during which the surviving counterparty is obtaining quotes from swap dealers. This would write:

$$H\frac{V_{A,k}^A(t_i)}{PV_A^A(t_i)} + \Delta^- PV_{A,k}^A(t_i) \tag{87}$$

If the (negative) value of the portfolio $PV_A^A(t_i)$ is above Threshold at the time of default: $PV_A^A(t_i) \geq -H$, the exposure caused by the specific derivative is simply the value of this derivative at time t_i since it is not protected by collateral, which is:

$$V_{A,k}^A(t_i) \tag{88}$$

From the two cases discussed above, we can write:

$$\begin{aligned}
&NEE_{A,k}^A(t_i) = \\
&\mathbb{E}_t\left[1_{\left\{0\geq PV_{A,k}^A(t_i)\geq -H\right\}} D(t,t_i)V_{A,k}^A(t_i)\right] \text{ (if within Threshold0} \\
&+\mathbb{E}_t\left[1_{\left\{-H>PV_{A,k}^A(t_i)\right\}} D(t,t_i+\Delta t)H\frac{\Delta^- PV_{A,k}^A(t_i)}{LGD_A}\right] \\
&\qquad\qquad \text{below Threshold} : \Delta V_{A,k}^A(t_i) \\
&+\mathbb{E}_t\left[1_{\left\{-H>PV_{A,k}^A(t_i)\right\}} D(t,t_i)H\frac{V_{A,k}^A(t_i)}{PV_A^A(t_i)}\right] \\
&\qquad \text{(below Threshold, pro} - \text{rata of gained Threshold)}
\end{aligned} \tag{89}$$

To complete the DVA calculation, we only have to weigh this Expected Exposure in the interval $[t_i, t_{i+1}]$ by the probability that default takes place in this interval, which is $PD_A(t_i, t_{i+1})$, and then sum over the date points t_i, and over all the N derivatives in the portfolio.

$$DVA_A^A(t) = \sum_{k=1}^{N} DVA_{A,k}^A(t) \tag{90}$$

With: $$DVA_{A,k}^A(t) = -LGD_A \sum_{t_i=t}^{T-1} PD_A(t_i, t_{i+1}) NEE_{A,k}^A(t_i) \tag{91}$$

One has to remember that in the mirror world of the DVA, the LGD_A represents a gain this time. Once we sum over the derivatives in the portfolio

$$DVA_A^A(t) = -LGD_A \sum_{k=1}^{N} \sum_{t_i=t}^{T-1} PD_A(t_i, t_{i+1}) NEE_{A,k}^A(t_i) \tag{92}$$

$$DVA_A^A(t) = -LGD_A \sum_{t_i=t}^{T-1} PD_A(t_i, t_{i+1}) NEE_A^A(t_i) \tag{93}$$

If we develop the Negative Expected Exposure, we can obtain an expression which remains relatively simple when we aggregate at portfolio's level (summing the *ks*).

$$DVA_A^A(t) = -LGD_A \sum_{t_i=t}^{T-1} PD_A(t_i, t_{i+1}) \mathbb{E}_t \Big[D(t, t_i) \{ \underbrace{\mathbb{1}_{\{0 \geq PV_A^A(t_i) \geq -H\}} (PV_A^A(t_i) + \Delta^- PV_{A,k}^A(t_i))}_{\text{If MtM within Threshold H, the Negative Expected Exposure is equal to MtM plus the negative variation over a ``reasonable period time''}} + \underbrace{\mathbb{1}_{\{-H > PV_A^A(t_i)\}} (-H + \Delta^- PV_{A,k}^A(t_i)}_{\text{If MtM is beyond Threshold the NEE is equal to: Threshold plus a negative variation over a ``reasonable period of time''}} \} \Big] \tag{94}$$

3.5.4 *DVA Formal Expression with Credit Risk on Collateral*

As was done for the CVA in paragraph 3.4.4., we now include the possibility of a default by A as a collateral receiving entity. The March 2015 margining regulation separates the "covered entities" (systematically important non-financial firms and financial firms) from the "non-covered entities." The former category benefits from an Initial Margin to be protected against a small variation during the short period after default during which the surviving entity obtains quotes for its claims (the "reasonable period of time"). This Initial Margin is also protected against default by being kept in a segregated account. The latter category ("non-covered entities"), on the other hand, remains unprotected.

This would lead to an expected loss we can write as:

$$-LGD_A \sum_{t_i=t}^{T-1} PD_A(t_i, t_{i+1}) \mathbb{E}_t \left[D(t, t_i) \{ \Delta^- PV_A^A(t_i) + H \} 1_{\{PV_A^A(t_i) > H\}} \right] \tag{95}$$

Remember that in this case A has a positive exposure and we are looking at a variation of the MtM after default, going beyond Threshold, which would put A in the situation of holding collateral in excess of the its positive MtM with counterparty B. This excess collateral becomes an exposure for B in case of a default by A. This would lead to adding an Expected Exposure term in the expressions of the DVA for "non-covered entities."

If we reintegrate this additional exposure into the DVA expression, we therefore obtain:

$$DVA_A^A(t) = -LGD_A \sum_{t_i=t}^{T-1} PD_A(t_i, t_{i+1})[NEE_A^A(t_i) - EE_B^A(t_i)] \qquad (96)$$

With:
- the discounted Expected Exposure term $EE_A^B(t_i)$ reflecting the potential credit loss on posted collateral for "non-covered entities":

$$NEE_A^A(t_i) = \mathbb{E}_t \left[D(t, t_i)\{1_{\{0 \geq PV_A^A(t_i) \geq -H\}} PV_A^A(t_i) + 1_{\{-H > PV_A^A(t_i)\}} H\}\right] \qquad (97)$$

For Basel covered entities

And for non-covered entities:

$$\begin{aligned} NEE_A^A(t_i) =& \mathbb{E}_t \Big[D(t, t_i)\{1_{\{0 \geq PV_A^A(t_i) \geq -H\}} (PV_A^A(t_i) + \Delta^- PV_A^A(t_i)) \\ &+ 1_{\{-H > PV_A^A(t_i)\}} (H + \Delta^- PV_A^A(t_i))\}\Big] \end{aligned} \qquad (98)$$

$$EE_B^A(t_i) = \mathbb{E}_t \left[D(t, t_i) Min\{0; \Delta^- PV_A^A(t_i) + H\} 1_{\{PV_A^A(t_i) > H\}}\right] \qquad (99)$$

3.6 *Bilateral CVA*

We conclude the two sections above by integrating the adjustments for default risk of the two counterparties—A and B—to the derivative contract in a formula that will reflect the bilateral nature of the derivative contract.

We now assume that both A and B can default and we look for the default-risk-adjusted value of the derivative: $V_A^{AB}(t)$. The superscript AB indicates that both A and B may default while the subscript A indicates that the valuation is calculated seen from the standpoint of A.

We start again from the standard default-risk-free valuation formula, seen from A, for the derivative: $V_A(t) = \mathbb{E}_t[C_A(t, T)]$, but this time we have to split the expectation among the three complementary events:

(i) $\{Min(\tau_A, \tau_B) > T\}$; no default either from A or B before the maturity of the derivative;
(ii) $\{\tau_B \leq Min(\tau_A, T)\}$; B defaults before the maturity of the derivative and defaults before A;
(iii) $\{\tau_A \leq Min(\tau_B, T)\}$; A defaults before the maturity of the derivative and defaults before B;

Under event (i), the expectation simply integrates the indicator function: $\mathbb{E}_t\left[1_{\{Min(\tau_A, \tau_B) > T\}} C_A(t, T)\right]$;

Under events (ii) and (iii), we follow the same reasoning as in the CVA and DVA analysis, respectively.

We have therefore the derivative pricing formula adjusted for bilateral credit risk—or with bilateral credit valuation adjustment—which includes both the CVA and the DVA:

$$\begin{aligned} V_A^{AB}(t) &= \mathbb{E}_t\left[1_{\{Min(\tau_A, \tau_B) > T\}} C_A(t, T)\right] \\ &+ \mathbb{E}_t\left[1_{\{\tau_B \leq Min(\tau_A, T)\}}[C_A(t, \tau_B) + D(t, \tau_B)\{R_B(V_A(\tau_B))^+ - (-V_A(\tau_B))^+\}]\right] \\ &+ \mathbb{E}_t\left[1_{\tau_A \leq Min(\tau_B, T)}[C_A(t, \tau_A) + D(t, \tau_A)\{(V_A(\tau_A))^+ - R_A(-V_A(\tau_A))^+\}]\right] \end{aligned} \tag{100}$$

With the same algebra as in the paragraphs on CVA and DVA above, we can derive the simpler expression:

$$V_A^{AB}(t) = V_A(t) + CVA_A^B(t) + DVA_A^A(t) \tag{101}$$

With:

$$\begin{aligned} CVA_A^B(t) &= -LGD_B \mathbb{E}_t\left[1_{\{\tau_B \leq Min(\tau_A, T)\}} D(t, \tau_B)(V_A(\tau_B))^+\right] \\ DVA_A^A(t) &= LGD_A \mathbb{E}_t\left[1_{\{\tau_A \leq Min(\tau_B, T)\}} D(t, \tau_A)(V_A(\tau_A))^+\right] \end{aligned}$$

If we now move to a discretized time frame and we further assume that the default time on A is independent from the default time on B, we would find the expression:

$$V_A^{AB}(t) = V_A(t) + CVA_A^B(t) + DVA_A^A(t) \tag{102}$$

$$CVA_A^B(t) = -LGD_B \sum_{t_i=t}^{T-1} PD_B(t_i, t_{i+1})[1 - PD_A(t_i, t_{i+1})]\left[EE_A^B(t_i) - NEE_A^B(t_i)\right] \tag{103}$$

$$DVA_A^A(t) = -LGD_A \sum_{t_i=t}^{T-1} PD_A(t_i, t_{i+1})[1 - PD_B(t_i, t_{i+1})][NEE_A^A(t_i) - EE_B^A(t_i) \tag{104}$$

The forms taken by $EE_A^B(t_i)$ and $EE_A^A(t_i)$ under a CSA with credit risk on collateral would then be the expressions previously found in the CVA and DVA formula derivations.

With the following expressions,

For Basel-covered entities:

$$EE_A^B(t_i) = \mathbb{E}_t\left[D(t,t_i)\left\{1_{\{0 \le PV_A^B(t_i) \le H\}} PV_A^B(t_i) + 1_{\{H < PV_A^B(t_i)\}} H\right\}\right] \tag{105}$$

$$NEE_A^A(t_i) = \mathbb{E}_t\left[D(t,t_i)\left\{1_{\{0 \ge PV_A^A(t_i) \ge -H\}} PV_A^A(t_i) - 1_{\{-H > PV_A^A(t_i)\}} H\right\}\right] \tag{106}$$

For non-covered entities:

$$EE_A^B(t_i) = \mathbb{E}_t[D(t,t_i)$$
$$\left\{1_{\{0 \le PV_A^B(t_i) \le H\}}(PV_A^B(t_i) + \frac{\Delta^+ PV_A^B(t_i)}{LGD_B}) + 1_{\{H < PV_A^B(t_i)\}}\left(H + \frac{\Delta^+ PV_A^B(t_i)}{LGD_B}\right)\right\}\Bigg] \tag{107}$$

$$-NEE_A^B(t_i) = \mathbb{E}_t\left[D(t,t_i)\{\Delta^+ PV_A^B(t_i) - H\}1_{\{PV_A^B(t_i) < -H\}}\right] \tag{108}$$

$$\begin{aligned} NEE_A^A(t_i) =& \mathbb{E}_t\Big[D(t,t_i)\{1_{\{0 \ge PV_A^A(t_i) \ge -H\}}(PV_A^A(t_i) + \Delta^- PV_A^A(t_i)) \\ &+ 1_{\{-H > PV_A^A(t_i)\}}(-H + \Delta^- PV_A^A(t_i)\}\Big] \end{aligned} \tag{109}$$

$$EE_B^A(t_i) = \mathbb{E}_t\left[D(t,t_i)Min\{0; \left(\Delta^- PV_A^A(t_i) + H\right)\}1_{\{PV_A^A(t_i) > H\}}\right] \tag{110}$$

Notes

1. Our main reference is this paragraph is the 2010 article by Michael Pykhtin and Dan Rosen, published as a Finance and Economics Discussion paper by the federal Reserve Board, Washington D.C.
2. As recommended by the accounting norm FAS 157 (Financial Accounting Standard 157).
3. Most results in this section have been established and/or can be found papers such as those by: Bielecki and Rutowski (2001), Picould (2005), Brigo and Capponi (2008), and Gregory (2009).
4. We refer in particular to the framework exposed in the Heath–Jarrow–Morton (HJM) model.

Expanding Valuation Metrics: FVA and KVA

Abstract In their attempt to comprehensively reflect all the costs associated with derivatives, swap dealer banks have introduced the Funding Valuation Adjustment (FVA) and the Capital Value Adjustment (KVA). FVA is a measure of the funding costs associated with a derivative transaction or with a portfolio of derivatives (among them is the cost of funding collateral posting). FVA is still debated among banks, academics and accounting firms: shouldn't the pricing of a derivative, and of any asset held, not reflect the funding spread of its owner? Isn't the FVA another way to see the DVA? The KVA measures the transaction cost of regulatory capital requirements imposed on derivatives.

Keywords CCR capital charge · CEM current exposure method ECE expected economic capital · Economic capital · FBA funding benefit adjustment · FCA funding cost adjustment · FVA funding value adjustment · IFRS · IMM internal model method · OIS overnight interest swap · Regulatory capital · ROC return on capital · Ted spread

1 Funding Value Adjustment: FVA

The Funding Value Adjustment (FVA) is an adjustment to the risk-neutral and no-default price of a derivative or of a derivatives portfolio, introduced by several dealer banks after 2008. While the CVA and the DVA metrics have been gradually added to derivative valuation in the

I. Zelenko, *Credit Risk Management for Derivatives*,
DOI 10.1007/978-3-319-57975-7_5

early years of the 2000 decade, as a necessary inclusion of credit risk in pricing, the FVA concept emerged in the aftermath of the 2007-08 crisis, as funding markets and funding conditions for banks were drastically altered. After 2008, dealer banks had become keenly aware of the need to manage and control funding costs arising from with derivatives trading. The FVA was born from internal transfer price rules within banks, established between the Treasury department, responsible for funding, and derivative trading desks, so as to convey to the latter a clear and readable monetary incentive to minimize funding needs. Industry practice then brought the FVA as another adjustment, alongside the CVA and the DVA, to derivative price.

$$V = V_{ND} + CVA + DVA + FVA \tag{I}$$

However, the FVA add-on is not unanimously accepted. There is not a standard and generally accepted definition, each bank has its own way of estimating it. The FVA concept has also been disputed by finance academics and accounting experts. For academics, the FVA is not consistent with derivative pricing theory. In particular, the inclusion of the cost of funds of the entity holding the derivative is very controversial, for the price of a market instrument should only reflect its risk.

Since the appearance of the FVA, market practitioners, academics, and accounting firms have been engaged in a vigorous, difficult, and still ongoing debate. Without going too deeply into this discussion, we will successively present in this chapter: (i) the background surrounding the elaboration of the FVA by dealer banks; (ii) the specific issue of funding collateral posting; (iii) the conceptual and practical issues raised by theory and accounting; and (iv) a concrete FVA formula and its relation to the CVA and DVA metrics.

1.1 FVA: Definition and Background

An essential piece of background comes from the pivotal role played by dealer banks in OTC derivative markets. Dealers are counterparties to all end users. They are almost solely responsible for market liquidity. Actual executable derivative prices result from dealer's ability to hedge risk and from the dynamics of competition. But pricing must also make derivatives trading a viable business proposition.

Prior to 2007, market practice among derivatives dealer banks was to value swaps and derivatives using the Libor curve. Libor was not exactly a risk-free rate (that is default-free rate) since it reflected the credit risk on short-term unsecured borrowing from banks. On the other hand though, banks could easily borrow and lend at the Libor rate, on the interbank market. The Libor rate used for easy and immediate access to funding or lending was very akin to the instantaneous text book risk-free rate. Moreover, the average credit quality of large dealers was stronger than it is now, and swaps were fully collateralized on the interdealer market. The 3-month Libor rate less the 3-month Treasury bill rate (the *Ted spread*) traded within the 50 basis points range under normal market conditions. All this meant that Libor could be considered as a reasonably good risk-free rate proxy. It was also a practical one. For interest rate swaps indexed on Libor, the use of the Libor rate had the added benefit of always keeping the floating leg close to par.

But the crisis profoundly disrupted the Libor market: The *Ted spread* reached a peak of 450 basis points in the fall of 2008; at the same time, most dealer banks could no longer borrow at Libor but materially above; the Libor rate could not continue to be seen as representative of the borrowing costs on the interbank market. In the end, Libor was discontinued as a risk-free proxy and replaced with the OIS curve for derivatives valuation.

In this context, dealer banks became much more aware, in their derivative activities, of the impact of their borrowing costs. Since they could no longer borrow at Libor, the pricing models they were using, and their Libor discount curve, were no longer reflecting their actual funding costs.

The cost of funding collateral, or more broadly, the cost of funding assets associated with derivatives positions (hedging portfolios) had to be revisited with a new crucial input: the funding spread of the bank relative to the new risk-free rate—the OIS (or its European equivalent, the EONIA).

The FVA is an adjustment by dealer banks to the value of a derivative position to reflect funding costs not included in standard pricing models, in particular the cost of funding collateral requirements. Citibank (see Box 1 below) gives a clear rationale for applying the FVA.

Box 1: Citibank Annual Report 2015. Statement on FVA

Note 25 to Financial Statements, page 250

Credit valuation adjustments (CVA) and, effective in the third quarter of 2014, funding valuation adjustments (FVA), are applied to over-the-counter (OTC) derivative instruments in which the base valuation generally discounts expected cash flows using the relevant base interest rate curve for the currency of the derivative (e.g., LIBOR for uncollateralized U.S.- dollar derivatives).

(...) **FVA reflects a market funding risk premium inherent in the uncollateralized portion of derivative portfolios, and in collateralized derivatives where the terms of the agreement do not permit the reuse of the collateral received.**

(...) The CVA and FVA are designed to incorporate a market view of the credit and funding risk, respectively, inherent in the derivative portfolio. However, most unsecured derivative instruments are negotiated bilateral contracts and are not commonly transferred to third parties. Derivative instruments are normally settled contractually or, if terminated early, are terminated at a value negotiated bilaterally between the counterparties. Thus, the CVA and FVA may not be realized upon a settlement or termination in the normal course of business.

1.2 FVA and the Cost of Funding Collateral

One of the main objectives of the FVA is to recover the funding costs associated with collateral, which may be particularly prominent for dealers and FVA as evidenced by the Citibank note in Box 1 above.

One may easily grasp how funding costs arise for dealers by considering that, except when they wish to create an open position for their own account, dealers would fully hedge themselves using basic products, either in the interdealer market or on exchanges. But derivative positions are fully collateralized on exchanges and among dealers. Given that the portfolio with the end user is fully hedged, the collateral paid to or received from the end user should match the collateral paid to or received from the interdealer market (see Fig. 1). We saw in Chap. "Restating the Role of Collateral" on collateral how, and under what conditions, the reuse of collateral, akin to the circulation of money, was supporting the liquidity of the derivatives market by reducing the cost of funding collateral to dealers. There are two situations, however, when this natural collateral transmission channel is broken (see Fig. 1):

- **The end user client has a CSA preventing them from posting collateral ("one-way collateral") or a CSA with very high**

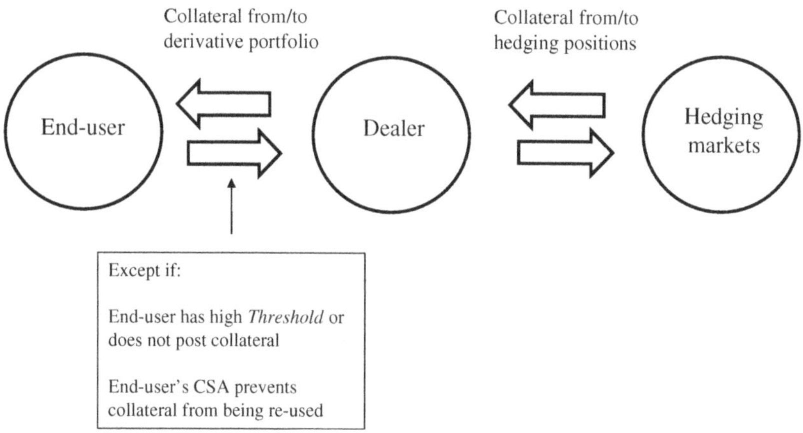

Fig. 1 Collateral funding (or non-funding) in a fully hedged position

Threshold and, as a result, does not post collateral: this is less frequent as collateral posting becomes more widespread (see Chap. "Restating the Role of Collateral"); it is still the norm for most governments and multilateral banks;
- **The dealer's client has a CSA which prevents the dealer from reusing collateral received**, be it cash or securities (see Chap. "Restating the Role of Collateral" and the paragraph on re-hypothecation).

Figure 1 is a convenient way to come to terms with the FVA seen as a cost of funding collateral in uncollateralized or imperfectly collateralized trades. It helps understand why the FVA is measured relative to perfect collateralization, a situation in which, at all times, collateral perfectly matches the exposure (positive MtM). Figure 1 also helps to distinguish the two sides of the FVA (for the FVA can also be a benefit): the *Funding Cost Adjustment* (FCA) and the *Funding Benefit Adjustment* (FBA).

FVA would be a cost, a FCA if: the dealer does not receive collateral from the end user while having to fund collateral to be paid in the hedge. This creates a net funding cost to the dealer, measured by its funding spread relative to the instantaneous risk-free rate. Let us take the example of a US dollar swap. The proxy for the risk-free rate is the OIS, derived from the Federal Funds rate, the overnight unsecured borrowing rate in the Fed Funds market where banks lend or borrow their excess or deficit in reserves with the Fed. On the collateral it has posted, he dealer is paid the Federal Funds rate, or the OIS. The fraction of this posted collateral that was not received may be borrowed in the Federal Funds market, at the OIS rate. In that case, there is no extra cost to the dealer. The post-2008 reality for dealer banks, however, is that their overall cost of funding, which averages the cost of all sources of funds, is distinctly above the OIS. The FCA will be computed as the dealer's funding spread relative to OIS multiplied by the size of this net funding need.

FVA would be a benefit however, a FBA, if the dealer receives collateral from the perfectly collateralized hedges of an uncollateralized portfolio with an end user. The dealer receives collateral, on which it pays the Fed Funds, the OIS, but this collateral does not have to be re-posted with the end user. It is a net source of funding at the risk-free rate (OIS), with no funding spread. In that sense, it is a funding benefit to the dealer, the FBA, and it is measured, by the dealer's overall funding spread relative to OIS times the volume of this collateral received. It is measured with the same spread (actual funding spread minus OIS) as the FCA as it is firstly seen as a reduction of the FCA.

$$FVA = FCA + FBA \tag{II}$$

1.3 The FVA Debate

At the heart of the FVA debate lays the fact that incorporating to the derivative price the funding spread of the entity holding the derivative is controversial from the points of view of accounting and finance theory.

As banks were seeing their funding rates deviating more noticeably and more durably from government rates and what could be accepted as risk-free rates, they have been led to reflect their borrowing costs in pricing, via the FVA. At the same time, their quantitative teams of dealer banks have attempted to revisit the traditional arbitrage-based derivative pricing models such as those of Merton or Black and Scholes, adding to them a new input, a new determinant of pricing: the funding cost, the cost of financing cash holdings associated with trading and arbitrage. The works of Vladimir Piterbarg, Christoph Burgard, and Mats Kjaer, working with Barclays and publishing in 2009-2011,[1] represented key references.

A first important preliminary remark should be about the variety of choices and decisions banks have to make in estimating the FVA. The result is the lack of standardization in the FVA calculation. For instance, Treasury bonds or liquid stocks that could be funded via repo at the repo rate, a risk-free rate very close to the OIS, would not justify a FVA, since such instruments can be funded at the risk free, as in the arbitrage-based textbook pricing model. But there are many types of underlying assets that would not necessarily offer an easy access to the repo market.

Academics such as John Hull and Alan White[2] have defined the FVA, as "an adjustment of the value of a derivative or a derivative portfolio to ensure that a dealer recovers its average funding costs when it trades and hedges derivatives" and have then argued it should be treated with great caution: "Theoretical arguments indicate that the dealer's valuation should not recover the whole of its funding costs."[3]

There is a general rule in finance theory: The valuation of financial instruments or projects should only reflect their risk, and not the funding spread of the firm holding them. Otherwise, this might lead to flawed decision making on risk and asset allocations: what to think for instance of a bank valuing Treasury bonds based on its own spread, and which might therefore never hold Treasury bonds in a debt-funded portfolio.

Accounting firms, from their end, have an imperative need for an unequivocal and constant definition of *fair value*: the MtM of a derivative contract should not change if it is transferred from one balance sheet to another. The definition of fair value in the IFRS states that "fair value is a market-based instrument, not an entity-specific measurement". Accounting firms recognize the DVA as being the market price of one's own default risk in a derivative contract: Counterparty Credit Risk in derivatives is indeed bilateral. As the market price of default risk, with a credit spread observable in CDS markets, for instance, the DVA can be added to the valuation. The FVA, however, is not a market risk measure of credit risk and is entity-specific.

Another troubling consequence of using the FVA in practice is that it may lead to arbitrage. The following example is inspired from the Hull and White 2014 paper. Assuming: a financial institution (A) with a low funding rate, close enough to the risk free rate (say 2%) buying an uncollateralized 1-year stock option with strike \$100 from a dealer bank (B) with a higher funding rate (say 4%), deducting both the DVA and the FVA from the Black-Scholes risk-free no default value (say $V = \$13$). DVA and FVA are both equal to \$0.5. Without collateral, A does not include FVA but would have to support the CVA (= \$0.5), as a cost, in order to hedge the default risk on B. A trades if the selling price is

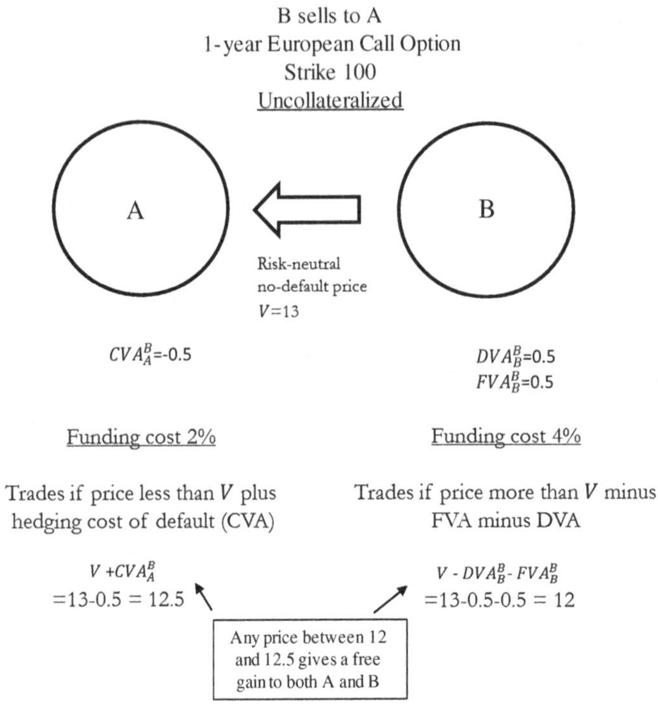

Fig. 2 Example of arbitrage in the presence of FVA and DVA adjustments

less than 13-0.5 = \$12.5. But B would trade if the price is more than 13-DVA-FVA = \$12. A price of \$12.25 would provide both A and B with a risk-free arbitrage profit (see Fig. 2).

Where does this leave us?

Let us consider the case of a swap. Let us consider a counterparty pricing the swap from its side. Let us suppose that the value of the swap is negative and is not collateralized. The risk of default of this counterparty—and its associated credit spread—can be incorporated into the price as an add-on, via the DVA. So, isn't the FVA, when a funding benefit—or a FBA—already counted via the DVA? There seems to be an agreement that the answer is yes.[4] And the formal expressions of DVA and FBA can be shown to equal each other (see below). So, when the exposure in a swap is negative, the swap produces a DVA gain to the counterparty, which can be alternatively understood, measured, and more importantly realized, as a FBA. DVA and FBA happen to be identical.

On the other hand, in the case of an uncollateralized exposure that is positive, which produces a CVA, and also a negative FVA—or a FCA (since the counterparty does not receive collateral), the bank would charge the FVA and incorporate it to the derivative pricing, as it cannot be recouped otherwise. The extra funding cost (measured as a spread relative to OIS) on the money borrowed to post-collateral that is not received from the end user but yet requested in the hedging portfolio, this cost could be recouped, accounting wise, by a DVA gain. However, it is not clear how the trading desk and the bank would actually realize this gain. So it looks likely the bank will continue to apply a FCA and operate with the following formula for adjustments:

$$V = V_{ND} + CVA + DVA + FCA \tag{III}$$

In their recent 2014 publication, Hull and White also find another case in which the FVA has to be added to the DVA and cannot be considered already counted in the DVA: "an FVA is justifiable only for the part of a company's credit spread that does not reflect default risk".

The FVA debate continues and the FVA, as a concept and as market practice, is still being elaborated. As the 2015 Basel regulations on the margining of uncleared OTC derivatives will make collateral more effective and widespread, the funding costs associated with imperfect collateralization may abate and the FVA become less essential.

1.4 A FVA Formula

We set ourselves in the perspective of the previous paragraph, using the full set of adjustments as outlined in:

$$V = V_{ND} + CVA + DVA + FCA \tag{IV}$$

To emphasize the links and differences between the three terms, we use the formulae for CVA and DVA laid out in Chap. "Adjusting for Credit and Debt Value: CVA and DVA". We use the formulae without credit risk on collateral.

$$CVA_A^B(t) = -LGD_B \sum_{t_i=t}^{T-1} PD_B(t_i, t_{i+1}) EE_A^B(t_i) \tag{V}$$

$$DVA_A^A(t) = -LGD_A \sum_{t_i=t}^{T-1} PD_A(t_i, t_{i+1}) NEE_A^A(t_i) \tag{VI}$$

$$FVA_A^B(t) = -\sum_{t_i=t}^{T-1} Spr_i(t_{i+1} - t_i) EE_A^B(t_i) \tag{VII}$$

where

- $EE_A^B(t_i)$ is the exposure net of collateral (or uncollateralized exposure) at t_i;
- Spr_i is the funding spread of A above the risk-free rate applicable to the time interval (t_i, t_{i+1})

2 Capital Charge and KVA

Banks and other financial institutions allocate economic capital or risk capital to their derivatives activities. Economic capital would be typically measured as the worst loss, obtained from a Value-at-Risk (VaR) and from a Credit VaR. This measure of risk also represents the fraction of the bank's equity that has been "allocated" to the derivatives activity. In corporate management logic, such equity should return a profit, at least equal to the target set by the firm for its return on equity. This rate of return becomes an additional element in the pricing of derivatives, the capital value adjustment or KVA.

Like the FVA, the KVA is not part of the finance theory textbook on derivatives. However, this is a much more familiar notion of the regulatory bodies.

After Basel I, in the 1980s and 1990s, the Basel Committee issued recommendations pertaining to loan pricing, based on the separation of the Expected Loss and the Unexpected Loss due to Credit Risk. Loan pricing was adding to the government bond rate of the maturity of the loan, a spread equivalent to the expected loss, a margin to cover costs, and the rate of remuneration of the Regulatory Capital (unexpected loss) allocated to the loan. Banks could use their own internal Economic Capital system as long as loan spreads were large enough to a positive rate of return to the Regulatory Capital.

Whereas the CVA is the derivative equivalent of the Expected Loss in loans, the KVA is the equivalent of the fraction of the lending spread destined to pay a remuneration to Economic (and Regulatory) Capital.

We start by going over the Regulatory Capital requirements that apply to derivatives (i). By projecting these capital requirements over the life of a derivative, or a derivative portfolio, we can produce a KVA formula (ii).

2.1 *Capital Requirements for Derivatives Counterparty Credit Risk*

Derivatives are subject to regulatory capital requirements, both for Market Risk and Counterparty Credit Risk (or Credit Risk as being specific to derivatives). These requirements have been notably reinforced in the aftermath of the 2008 crisis, at the request of the G20, and have been coordinated within the Basel III framework.

Market Risk requirements for derivatives would be part of an overall formula relying on 10-day Value-at-Risk (VaR), if an internal model exists, or a standard formula, designed to replicate the VaR calculations.

Counterparty Credit Risk (CCR) requirements for derivatives have been initially laid out in a specific document of the Basel II regulatory compendium[5]; these requirements have then been reinforced and expanded by Basel III. Under Basel, there are three calculation methods for CCR:

- Current Exposure Method (CEM), which applies to banks that do not qualify to use internal models;
- Standardized Approach, for banks that cannot use an internal model, but wish to use measures of risk that reflect better the risk on their portfolio;
- Internal Model Method: Banks can use their internal Credit VaR model, once it is validated by the supervisory authorities.

The simpler approach, the CEM, would rely on an instantaneous measure of the derivative netting set's exposure, using the PFE or Potential Financial Exposure), multiplied by the Basel Risk Weight (RW) of the counterparty, multiplied by 8% (the Basel Capital Ratio).

CCR Capital Charge (CEM) = [Replacement Cost (MtM) + PFE − Volatility Adjusted Collateral]*RW*8%

The IMM would rely on values of the positive Expected Exposure (EE) for the netting set, over a series of time intervals in the future.

Regulators recommend to use conservative metrics derived from the EE curve. Economic or Regulatory Capital will consist of a worst-case estimate of a credit loss, over the time horizon of the derivatives' portfolio, the netting set, at the 99.9% confidence level (Basel requirement) or at higher confidence levels (a AAA rating would require a 99.97% level in a purely quantitatively based rating setup).

The EE curve can also serve as input to a calculation of future Economic or Regulatory Capital needs, and their associated costs. The bank can then factor the present value of these costs into its pricing.

2.2 KVA Formula

Based on the above, we can propose the following formula for computing the KVA (see Fig. 3).

$$KVA_A^B(t) = -\sum_{t_i=t}^{T} ROC(t_{i+1} - t_i)ECE_A^B(t_i) \tag{I}$$

With:

KVA_A^B : Capital Value Adjustment due to the exposure on B, seen from A, based on the Expected Economic Capital used by B over the life of the netting set;

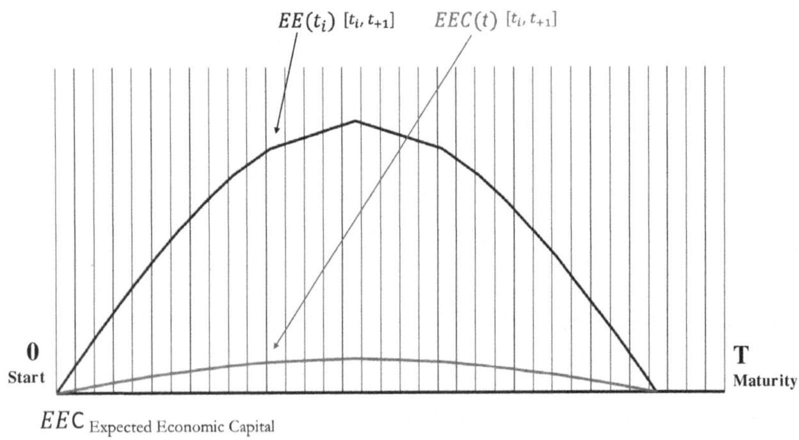

Fig. 3 Expected Exposure and Expected Economic Capital

ECE_A^B : Expected Economic Capital discounted at time t, due to the exposure on B, seen from A, based on the Expected Exposure, computed at all future intervals $[t_i, t_{i+1}]$;

ROC : Return on Capital required by firm A on its derivatives activities.

Notes

1. Piterbarg: "Funding beyond Discounting: Collateral Agreements and Derivatives Pricing," Risk, 2010; Burgard and Kjaer: "In the Balance," Risk, 2011; Partial differential equation representation of derivatives with counterparty risk and funding costs, The Journal of Credit Risk, 2011 (Piterbarg 2010).
2. Among the main contributions to the debate are: Hull and White: "Valuing Derivatives: Funding Value Adjustments and Fair Value", Financial Analysts Journal, vol. 70, N.3, 2014; Hull and White: "The FVA Debate", Risk, 25th anniversary edition, 2012; Piterbarg (Hull and White 2014; 2012) (mentioned above); Burgard and Kjaer (mentioned above);
3. Hull and White: "Valuing Derivatives: Funding Value Adjustments and Fair Value", Financial Analysts Journal, vol. 70, N.3, 2014 (Hull and White 2014)
4. For a formal proof of the double counting, see Massimo Morini and Andrea Prampolini: "Risky funding: a unified framework for counterparty and liquidity charges," Working Paper, 2010.
5. The Application of Basel II to Trading Activities and the Treatment of Double Default Effects, Basel Committee on Banking Supervision, July 2005.

References

Hull, J., & White, A. (2012, October). The FVA debate continues: Hull and white respond to their critics. *Risk.*

Hull, J., & White, A. (2014). Valuing derivatives: Funding value adjustments and fair value. *Financial Analysts Journal.*

Piterbarg, V. (2010, February). Funding beyond discounting: Collateral agreements and derivatives pricing. *Risk-magazine.net.*

Bibliography

Alavian, S., Ding, J., Whitehead, P., & Laudicina, L. (2010, October). *Credit valuation adjustment.*

Albanese, C., & Iabichino, S. (2013). *The FVA-DVA puzzle: Risk management and collateral trading strategies.* Working Paper.

Albanese, C., Andersen, L., & Iabichino, S. (2015, January). *FVA accounting, risk management and collateral trading*, Risk.

Andersen, L., Duffie, D., and Song, Y. (2016, March). *Funding Value Adjustments*, Extremely Preliminary Draft.

Andersen, L., Pykhtin, M., & Sokol, A. (2016, January). *Rethinking margin period of risk.* Retrieved from SSRN: https://ssrn.com/abstract=2719964.

Anderson, R., & Joeveer, K. (2014). *The economics of collateral.* London School of Economics.

BCBS, IOSCO. (2015, March). *Margin requirements for non-centrally cleared derivatives.*

BCBS. (2006, June). *International convergence of capital measurement and capital standards, a revised framework—Comprehensive version.*

BCBS. (2012, December). *Basel III counterparty credit risk and exposures to central counterparties—Frequently asked questions.*

BCBS. (2014, August). *Foundations of the standardized approach for measuring counterparty credit risk exposures.* Working Paper No 26.

BCBS. (2014, March). *The standardized approach for measuring counterparty credit risk exposures.*

BCBS. (2016, March). *Literature review on integration of regulatory capital and liquidity instruments.* WP 30.

Bielecki, T., Jeanblanc, M., & Rutkowski, M. (2004, May). *Pricing of defaultable claims.* Princeton Lectures on Mathematical Finance.

I. Zelenko, *Credit Risk Management for Derivatives*,
DOI 10.1007/978-3-319-57975-7

BIS. (2015, November). *Statistical release, OTC derivatives statistics at end-June 2015, monetary and economic department.*

BIS. (2016, September). *Triennal central bank survey, OTC interest rate derivatives turnover in April 2016.* Monetary and Economic Department.

Bliss, R., & Kaufman, G. (2005). *Derivatives and systemic risk: Netting, collateral, and closeout.* Federal Reserve Bank of Chicago WP 2005–03.

Bomfim, A. (2002). *Counterparty credit risk in interest rate swaps during times of market stress.* Washington, DC: Federal Reserve Board.

Brace, A., Gatarek, D., and Musiela, M. (1997). The market model of interest rate dynamics. *Mathematical Finance, 7*(2).

Brigo, D., & Masetti, M. (2005). Risk neutral pricing of counterparty risk. In M. Pykhtin (Ed.). *Counterparty credit risk modeling.* London: Risk books.

Brigo, D., & Morini, M. (2010). *Dangers of bilateral counterparty risk: the fundamental impact of closeout conventions.* Working Paper.

Brigo, D., Buescu, C., & Morini M. (2011). *Impact of the first to default time on bilateral CVA*, draft version June 2011.

Brigo, D., Morini, M., & Pallavicini, A. (2013, April). *Counterparty credit risk, collateral and funding.* UK: Wiley.

Burgard, C., & Kjaer, M. (2013, December). *Funding strategies, funding costs*, Risk.

Burgard, C., &Kjaer, M. (2012). *A generalized CVA with funding and collateral.* Working Paper.

Carver, L. (2012). Capital or P&L? Deutsche Bank losses highlight CVA trade-off. *Risk.net.* Retrived from October 2013.

Collin-Dufresne, P., & Solnik, B. (2001). On the term structure of default premia in the swap and LIBOR markets. *Journal of Finance, 56.*

Collin-Dufresne, P., Goldstein, R., & Martin, J. (2001). The determinants of credit spread changes. *Journal of Finance, 56.*

Cox, J., Ingersoll, J., & Ross, S. (1981). The relation between forward prices and futures prices. *Journal of Financial Economics, 9.*

Crepey, S., Albanese, C., & Caenazzo, S. (2016). Capital valuation adjustment and funding valuation adjustment. *ASQF Conference,* June 2016.

Duffie, D., & Singleton, K. (1997). An econometric model of the term structure of interest-rate swap yields. *Journal of Finance, 52.*

Edwards, F. (1995). Derivatives can be hazardous to your health: The case of Metallgesellschaft. *Derivatives Quarterly, 1*(3, Spring).

European Banking Agency (EBA). (2015, February). *Report on Credit Valuation Adjustment (CVA) under Article 456 (2) of Regulation (EU) 575/2013.*

Felson, D., Kelly, R., & Wiemert, A. (2004). *Metallgesellschaft. AG: A case study.* Illinois Institute of Technology.

Financial Times. (2015, December 10). *CME losing ground to LCH. Clearnet in swaps clearing battle*, by Joe Rennison.

Fleming, M., & Schmidt, A. (2014). The failure resolution of Lehman brothers. *Federal Reserve Bank of New York Review*, December 2010.

Frankel, A., & Palmer, D. (1996, August). *The case of Metallgesellschaft*. BoG of the Federal Reserve (Discussion Paper No 560).

FSB. (2015). *Sixth progress report on the implementation of the G-20 data gaps initiative*. Prepared by the Staff of the IMF and the FSB Secretariat.

FSB. (2015, October). *Reporting financial transactions to trade repositories in the Americas*.

Fuji, M., & Takahashi, A. (2011, January). *Choice of collateral currency. Risk, 24*.

Gordy, M., & Marrone, J. (2010, June). *Granularity adjustments for mark-to-market credit risk models*. Washington, DC: Federal Reserve Board.

Green, A., & Kenyon, C. (2016, March). Accounting for KVA under IFRS 13. *Risk*.

Green, A., Kenyon, C., & Dennis, C. (2014, December). KVA: Capital valuation adjustment. *Risk*.

Gregory, J. (2012). *Counterparty credit risk and credit value adjustment,: A continuing challenge for global financial markets*. UK: Wiley.

Gregory, J., & German, I. (2012). *Closing out DVA*. Working Paper.

Grinblatt, M. (1995). *An analytic solution for interest-rate swap spreads*. Yale University Working Paper.

Heath, D., Jarrow, R., and Morton, A. (1992). *Bond Pricing and the Term Structure of Interest Rates, Econometrica, 60*(1), January 1992.

Hull, J. (2010, April). *OTC derivatives and central clearing: Can all transactions be cleared?* Working Paper.

Hull, J., Sokol, A., & White, A. (2014, June). *Modeling the short rate: the real and risk-neutral worlds*. Rotman School of Management, WP 2403067.

Infante, S. (2015, March). *Liquidity windfalls: The consequences of repo Rehypothecation*. Washington, DC: Federal Reserve Board.

ISDA. (2012, November). *Initial margin for non-centrally cleared swaps, understanding the systemic implications*.

ISDA. (2016, April 18). *Margin requirements for uncleared swaps—comparative chart*.

Kenyon, C., & Green, A. (2015). *Warehousing credit (CVA) risk, capital (KVA), and tax (TVA) consequences*. Working Paper.

Laughton, S., & Vaisbrot, A. (2012, September). In defense of FVA: A response to Hull and White. *Risk, 8*.

Maurin, V. (2014, March). *Re-using the collateral of others, a general equilibrium model of Rehypothecation*. European University Institute.

McDonald, R., & Paulson, A. (2014, October). *AIG in hindsight*. Federal Bank of Chicago WP 2014–07.

Mello, A., & Parsons, J. (1995). Maturity structure of a hedge matters: Lessons from the Metallgesellschaft debacle. *Journal of Applied Corporate Finance, 8*(1, Spring).

Miglietta, A., Picillo, C., & Pietrunti, M. (2015, October). The impact of CCPs' margin policies on repo markets (BIS WP 515).
Morini, M. (2015, February). *XVAs: Funding, credit, debit & capital in pricing.*
O'Kane, D. (2013). *Optimizing the compression cycle: Algorithms for multilateral netting in OTC derivatives markets.* Working Paper.
O'Kane, D., & Schlogl, L. (2001, February). *Modeling credit: Theory and practice.* Analytical Research Series. Lehman Brothers.
Pallavicini, A., Perini, D., & Brigo, D. (2011, December). *FVA: A consistent framework including CVA, DVA, collateral netting rules and re-hypthecation.*
Piterbarg, V. (2012a, July). Stuck with collateral. *Risk, 26*(11).
Piterbarg, V. (2012b, October). Cooking with collateral. *Risk, 8.*
Pykhtin, M. & Sokol, A. (2012). *Modeling credit exposure to systematically important counterparties.* Risk Minds Conference Amsterdam, December 2012.
Pykhtin, M. (2012). General wrong-way risk and stress calibration of exposure. *Financial Analysts Journal,* January 2016.
Pykhtin, M. (2012, July). Model foundations of the Basel III CVA standardized CVA charge. *Risk.*
Pykhtin, M., & Rosen D. (2010, October). *Pricing counterparty risk at trade level and CVA allocations.* Washington, DC: Federal Reserve Board.
Pykhtin, M., & Sokol, A. (2013). Systemic wrong-way risk. In F. Galizia (Ed.). *Managing systemic exposure.* London: Risk Books.
Pykhtin, M., & Zhu, S. (2006). Measuring counterparty credit risk for trading products under Basle II. In *Basel handbook,* 2nd ed. London: Risk Books.
Pykhtin, M., & Zhu, S. (2007, July/August). *A guide to modeling counterparty credit risk.* Global Association of Risk Professionals.
Risk. (2016). *Interview with Benoît Cœuré, member of the executive board of the ECB and chairman of the committee on payments and market infrastructures (CPMI).*
Singh, M. (2010). *Collateral netting and systemic risk in the OTC derivatives market.* IMF Working Paper WP/10/99.
Singh, M. (2013, January). *The changing collateral space.* IMF WP/13/25.
Singh, M. (2015, February). *Understanding the role of collateral in financial markets.* Brookings Institution.
Steigerwald, R., & DeCarlo, D. (2014). *Resolving CCPs after Dodd-Frank: Are CCPs eligible for `Orderly Liquidation'?* WP Fed. Res. Bank of Chicago.
Tucker, P. (2014). *Regulatory reform, stability, and central banking.* Hutchins Center on Fiscal and Monetary Policy at Brookings Institution.
Zhu, H. (2012). *Finding a good price in opaque over-the-counter markets.* Review of Financial Studies.

Index

I. Zelenko, *Credit Risk Management for Derivatives*,
DOI 10.1007/978-3-319-57975-7

The manufacturer's authorised representative in the EU is Springer Nature Customer Service Centre GmbH, Europaplatz 3, 69115 Heidelberg, Germany. If you have any concerns regarding our products, please contact ProductSafety@springernature.com

Printed and bound by CPI Group (UK) Ltd, Croydon, CR0 4YY

25/09/2026

02222890-0020